Psychoanalytic Work in East Africa

Psychoanalytic Work in East Africa presents a unique insight into psychoanalytic practice with urban populations in East Africa.

Barbara Saegesser describes her psychoanalytic work in different East African locations and in a wide range of contexts. Each chapter considers a particular context, from work in general hospitals and psychiatric hospitals and with children in orphanages, to maternity wards with women who have been subjected to genital mutilation. Saegesser reflects on questions of gender, religion and working across cultures throughout, and considers the benefits of this approach for people who have not previously encountered psychoanalysis.

Psychoanalytic Work in East Africa will be of great interest to psychoanalysts and psychoanalytic psychotherapists looking to learn more about working with people in complex, challenging or dangerous situations, across cultures, and in areas where psychoanalysis is not at all known.

Barbara Saegesser is a training analyst with the Swiss Psychoanalytical Society (Schweizerische Gesellschaft für Psychoanalyse – SGPsa) and also with the International Psychoanalytical Association (IPA). She was president of the commission treating ethical problems in the Swiss Society of Psychoanalysis among many other positions and has worked in East Africa since 2005 in a wide range of contexts, including orphanages, shelters, psychiatric hospitals and maternity wards.

IPA in the Community
Series editor: Harvey Schwartz

Recent titles in the Series include:

Applying Psychoanalysis in Medical Care
Edited by Harvey Schwartz

Trauma, Flight and Migration
Psychoanalytic Perspectives
Edited by Vivienne Elton, Marianne Leuzinger-Bohleber, Gertraud Schlesinger-Kipp and Vivian B. Pender

Psychoanalytic Work in East Africa
Barbara Saegesser

Psychoanalytic Work in East Africa

Barbara Saegesser

LONDON AND NEW YORK

Designed cover image: Getty | zeljkosantrac

First published 2025
by Routledge
4 Park Square, Milton Park, Abingdon, Oxon OX14 4RN

and by Routledge
605 Third Avenue, New York, NY 10158

Routledge is an imprint of the Taylor & Francis Group, an informa business

© 2025 Barbara Saegesser

The right of Barbara Saegesser to be identified as author of this work has been asserted in accordance with sections 77 and 78 of the Copyright, Designs and Patents Act 1988.

All rights reserved. No part of this book may be reprinted or reproduced or utilised in any form or by any electronic, mechanical, or other means, now known or hereafter invented, including photocopying and recording, or in any information storage or retrieval system, without permission in writing from the publishers.

Trademark notice: Product or corporate names may be trademarks or registered trademarks, and are used only for identification and explanation without intent to infringe.

British Library Cataloguing-in-Publication Data
A catalogue record for this book is available from the British Library

ISBN: 978-1-032-58809-4 (hbk)
ISBN: 978-1-032-58811-7 (pbk)
ISBN: 978-1-003-45158-7 (ebk)

DOI: 10.4324/9781003451587

Typeset in Palatino
by Apex CoVantage, LLC

This book is dedicated to my creative, beautiful, loving, charming and very intelligent mother, Marianne, who died in 1947.

I had extremely few years to live with her. Nevertheless, she gave me much of her own personality. I think she would have liked my East African psychoanalytical work and also my present book.

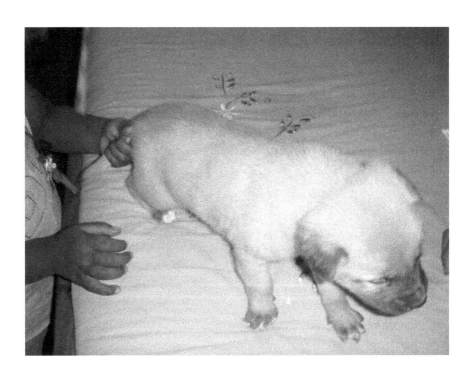

Contents

Preface   *viii*

1 Psychoanalytic work in East African cities   1

2 Psychoanalytic fieldwork in East African cities   12

3 Drop-in and home for street boys   17

4 Parenthood in East African cities   24

5 School systems and school visits in East African cities
   and rural areas   39

6 The baby and the child without a mother   49

7 Babies with their mothers   57

8 Sex/gender differences   66

9 The Quran, children's games and creative playing in
   the sands of El-Alamein   78

10 Concepts and treatments for psychosomatic patients
   in the East African environment   89

11 Free ambulatory choice of patients in the main room
   of the women's station   105

12 What is it that initiates inner and outer psychic
   change? What initiates a transformation process?   121

Index   *128*

Preface

I would like to begin by thanking the colleague and friend who gave me the chance to publish my psychoanalytic East African work. When I began telling Peter Bründl, Ph.D. (head of many editorial and psycho-analytic/psychodynamic activities and projects in Munich/Germany) about my psychoanalytical fieldwork in East Africa, he said to me, "Write something about it. You can publish it with us." He meant the publishing house Brandes & Apsel, of Munich, in whose *Jahrbuch der Kinder- und Jugendlichen-Psychoanalyse* (*Yearbook of Child and Adolescent Psychoanalysis*) parts of my work appeared from 2015 to 2023 (vols. 4–12, ed. Peter Bründl and Carl E. Scheidt, with different co-editors). Every year I had the chance to publish about my just-finished new work in East Africa. When writing for those volumes, I tried to address, at least to some extent, the special topic chosen by the annual *Jahrbuch* (Yearbook) as a focus for that particular volume, e.g. developmental issues, schools, parenthood, psychosomatic, gender difference etc. Sometimes I was able to contribute directly to the discussion of the topic; sometimes I could not, because the cultural differences to the Western world were too great.

My thanks go also to Sophie Klopfenstein, Master of TCM, Bienna (CH). She helped me when I could not find the way to complete the final digital structuration of my book.

At times, I think back almost in wonder at the luck and the courage on my part that enabled me to go to East Africa and to keep going again for quite a long time and find new places to work there. I was not attached by a contract to one of the big aid organisations. I worked alone, set on this path by my experiences in the one particular orphanage I met first. Working alone had the advantage that when the time came, I could get to where I wanted to be, quite quickly. One person working independently can gather information, orient herself, look, listen and think about what work might be important or interesting. Many times, I was recommended to another country and place; on one occasion I found my new working place by making enquiries at unlikely organisations that acted somewhat like placement agencies. It was unlikely in the sense that these organisations were mainly looking for young people, who wanted to get their first taste of different

Preface ix

kinds of work in East Africa, which did not really apply in my case. Anyway, I could find through them a very interesting geographic place and interesting institutions.

These days I have the chance to bring a lot of my East African working experiences back to life by reading the English translation of what I had written about my East African work over the years in the German language. It allows me to keep holding on to East Africa, and enables me to discover new aspects, new facets made visible by the distance. Naturally, as I'm writing about all this now, I would not write everything the same way as I did back then, nor would I probably act and react to the situations I described in just the same way. But in general, I often find myself astonished by the challenges I took on and where I took these on, how I approached them and, sometimes, that I was even able to bear them.

Since this present book is the summary of reports of my psychoanalytical working in different places and institutions in East Africa, for this reason they are written year by year and contain sometimes important repetition in the yearly report, especially concerning politics, religion and culture, as these three in Eastern Africa go completely together. Religion and politics do not work in isolation.

Several parts of this book I first wrote and edited in German. I have not changed fundamentally the way in which I first wrote this book in the German language. One can read isolated chapters and get also in this way the important information about religion, politics and culture, or one can read the whole book as one piece and find some repetitions. It's because of the special way I have written my book and how it has come together, which leads me to repeat central key points such as religion, politics and culture in various chapters. The reader is asked to adapt to these repetitions.

1 Psychoanalytic work in East African cities

At the end of 2005, I flew to Egypt to rest and look around for a few days. On the very first day, on my walk through a beautiful old park by the sea, almost deserted, I noticed a walking couple, husband and wife, accompanied step by step by a red cat, proudly walking alongside the couple, so to speak, with its tail raised. This rare sight, this image seemed so cheerful to me that I approached the couple and asked them if they would often go for a walk together with their cat. It is not every day that a cat accompanies its walking "master" in a demure and proud manner like a puppy. No, they replied, and they explained to me how unusual this morning was for them. They had just landed in Alexandria in the early hours of the morning after returning from Europe. The husband, a doctor, lives here. His wife is a teacher in England. Quickly we are talking, exchanging ideas standing up, until a phone call interrupts us. Doctor M. is asked to accompany a convoy to an orphanage. This conversation marks the beginning of some working relationships and friendships in a city where I previously knew no one. Thanks to the newly acquired acquaintance and doctor who was asked to help with the planned convoy, I was able to visit an orphanage the very next day with this convoy, bringing clothes and toys, Christmas presents, paid for from the proceeds of the annual bazaar of the city's wealthier ladies. Never before had I thought of visiting orphanages there. No, I wanted to look for and get to know the city full of artists that Lawrence Durrell brings to life in his "Alexandria Quartet" written in 1957–1960.

The convoy seems rather strange to me: four big cars packed with shoeboxes containing gifts for the orphans. Some of the original and extravagant initiators of the bazaar are elderly and it looks as if they are the wives of former English colonialist generals. In the home, the 100 or so shoeboxes, each of which is designed and put together for special age groups, are given to orphans of different ages, differentiated according to gender. And what do the orphans do? There are some who are happy and say thank you, others who accept the shoebox donations and then flee away again, and then there are those who do not come to the ladies and their shoebox donations at all. These are severely depressed, from the smallest to the largest – 3 to about

DOI: 10.4324/9781003451587-1

2   *Psychoanalytic work in East African cities*

16 years old – and their faces are old and withered from misery, sorrow and pain. They remain half-hidden at the back or crouched there against a wall that supports them a little from behind. Others turn and run away. They obviously expect nothing more from adults, their hopelessness seems bottomless. When I see these completely desperate, inwardly averted and probably utterly lonely orphans, who turn away from adults and run away, it becomes instantly evident to me that I would like to work psychotherapeutically in orphanages in this city. This cannot be done in the current home and I enquire about other orphanages. I am told that there are many. Two days later I start my work. Thus begins my years of psychoanalytical and educational work in East African Muslim cities and countries, in the orphanages.

The red cat in the old, magnificent park by the sea, walking next to its masters, leads to a new, exceedingly important facet of my life and working life.

So now I am doing humanitarian work in various East African countries in orphanages and hospitals during part of my holiday time afforded by my Swiss practice. I start in orphanages, then work in a home for street boys, then in orphanages and international organisations such as SOS Infants and Save the Children, here also providing rudimentary training functions and giving lectures, then in a large, this time Christian orphan organisation, then in a hospital for the very poorest.

I also work further south in a hospital for the very poor, then in maternity and neonatology, and finally in the East African South in the state psychiatric dependency and in the main hospital. In all these institutions, I go where the need is greatest – at least as far as I can tell. I choose my own place of work, for example in the maternity department in the Chambre du travail, critical births, operating theatres, waking rooms, hospital rooms or neonatology. In psychiatry, as soon as I get there, I am pointed to "difficult patients" and asked to "do something" with them. The patients are children, orphans with aunts or grandmothers, women, men, drug addicts, psychosomatically destroyed by drugs, malnutrition and daily misery. Their respective state of illness is much more miserable and dramatic compared to patients in Western European psychiatric clinics and hospitals.

Amid the great psychosomatic misery of children, the psychosomatic misery of adults as well as the psychosomatic misery of the caretakers of the various orphanages and hospitals, I have learned a lot about cultural and cultural-religious peculiarities of East African cities and ethnic groups and about small orphans, about adult war orphans and people threatened by hunger and fear and marked by psychosomatic misery, especially refugees (especially from Somalia, Sudan, Eritrea and Ethiopia), and at the same time learned to appreciate my psychoanalytical concepts and clinical experience as an indispensable basis for my new field of work in a new way. I am sometimes confronted with highly worrying forms of mental and psychosomatic illness and near-death conditions: I find myself exposed to these situations, so to speak.

Only after working for a while in East African cities and rural areas do I gradually realise more clearly that psychology is hardly known or practised in some places (at best it is used for measuring IQ), and psychotherapy of course even less so. I am getting used to bringing something foreign into the respective cultures or ethnic groups and into the understanding, into the self-understanding, of the individual or a family structure with my psychoanalytic attitude and my psychoanalytic thinking and assessment of configurations. So I am not only confronted with the mistrust that is felt towards white people who want to prescribe and "apply" something unknown – this can be reminiscent of the approach of the colonists – but at the same time with mistrust with regard to my way of approaching babies, children and adults, predominantly women, and working with them psychoanalytically. At that time, the term psychotherapy was not even known in the medical or home environment, not even in psychiatry.

In general, here, in East African areas, I experience how, despite cultural differences and difficulties, but being aware of these difficulties and carefully weighing what I share of my thoughts or not, people/patients begin to take an interest in themselves in a new way. Something starts to move.

The individual, subjective psychological is predominantly ignored in many East African cultures and ethnic groups. One's own psychological events are standardised according to the Quran, which apparently should and can regulate and fulfil all human individual-subjective and "objective" needs, including the psychological. Something "fundamentally" different happens through my work. I do not represent or advocate any Islamic ideology. With my occupation, the intensive therapeutic mirroring of especially my patients' most urgent subjective and narcissistic needs and individual needs, my reverie of the patients, and my personal psychoanalytical hypotheses about the psychic configurations of the patients, a "small freedom", something tiny and new, something rediscovered can possibly develop and unfold in the thinking of the patients. For example, the ability to discriminate or to perceive anew old familiar things in oneself, to unfold seemingly "unknown" longings and desires. And these new psychic qualities, actually rediscovered from the fund of the non-Islamic-normed world of children and the unconscious, do not correspond to the Quranic norms regarding the thinking and feeling of a (Muslim) human being.

I work in the environment described, which is somehow similar to working in an outpatient clinic. This seems to be qualitatively sufficient in terms of time and in the respective moment, and should perhaps remain so because of the tension between the special religious-social anchoring of the patients, doctors and helping persons and the psychoanalytical points of view and concepts that are controversial to this attitude and which I carefully introduce.

4 *Psychoanalytic work in East African cities*

Psychotherapeutic, let alone psychoanalytic active and passive work, as already mentioned, is hardly known in Islamic countries; at least this is true for those East African urban and rural areas that are more familiar to me. In my work I mainly meet Muslim people who have no idea about what I "do" psychoanalytically because they are not supposed to know. This is not only true for patients, but also for their environment. For my psychotherapeutic work, no basic carpet has already been laid, so to speak. I enter new territory and so do the patients with me.

From this point of view, it is particularly important for me to develop some considerations that relate to the interplay between the sphere of influence of the Quran and the sphere of influence of psychoanalytic thoughts and concepts. In the countries and cities in which I work, the Quran, in whatever formulation or interpretation, is regarded as the primer of life, as the guide to faith and life par excellence, for all aspects of life, quite specifically for everything and anything in everyday human life. These religious-worldly norms are socially extremely binding. They claim a validity and a control of the way of life of those concerned, as might have been the case with Christianity in most European societies, probably hundreds of years ago. Deviants, depending on their ethnicity – as we know – are sometimes punished in the most gruesome and cruel ways (expelled from their society, their ethnicity; hands or feet are chopped off; they are tortured, multiply tortured, stoned, killed). These religious and social norms remind me each time of sectarian norms found, even to this day, in Western European areas. An important part of the content of the faith says that the one who believes in another faith, i.e. the one who lives outside the one "chosen" religious community, outside the Islamic faith or the faith of the sect followers, is a bad, i.e. evil person who should not be contacted in any way. Manichaean thinking, acting and condemning prevail.

Now, right at the beginning of my psychoanalytic-psychotherapeutic conversations, I always come up against this rigid set of norms. For example, even seriously ill patients tell me that I'm doing well, that I'm doing very well today, that God wants it that way and so on. If things are not going well, the suffering and unhappiness are God's will and therefore also good. Whoever has no money to live on, no money to feed his family, does not therefore have to despair, because this is God's will and God will give a hint or show a way in which a little money or food can be found for the family. At the same time, the Quran forbids *joie de vivre* that does not specifically follow the rules of the Quran. I am referring to a form of *joie de vivre* that can be a positive part of life in many Western countries: joy, for example, in music (from classical to rock etc.), in theatre, in cultural actions, in love, in sexuality, without these having anything to do with religion in the strict sense. Joy per se is possibly granted to babies and children, perhaps even to men. I assume that the discussion and banter in the men's rooms give the participants joy and pleasure, as do the pleasure of being served by women or the pleasure of sexuality, which is deliberately made impossible for genitally mutilated women, and more.

Seen and understood psychoanalytically, this standardised human – also inner – attitude, these psychic Quranic armatures of the internalised Quran, configure an intense resistance that suffocates individual and subjective emotions, desires and thoughts, as it were, in the abundance of the Quranic commandments; as psychoanalytically understood this not only represses such emotions, desires and thoughts but tends to split them off. I am talking about a religious, ethnic and social resistance to seeing, understanding, uncovering and unfolding individual psychosomatic life and suffering that has grown and solidified over centuries. And breaking down this religiously anchored resistance and cultivating freer (liberated) thoughts and actions can become life-threatening. Only if I manage to go along with these defences – for example, in dealing with feelings of shame and guilt – not to diminish them, but to preserve the religious value, as it were, can I reach the suffering person, his self and his subjective psychic life, which he keeps enclosed, as in a crypt, behind the Islamic-religious, ethnic armature, so to speak. This normative-religious-social resistance has more power than, say, social norms in most Western societies. The bulwark of the fundamental resistance just described against a subjectification or another deep understanding of the individual is, as it were, tyrannical. If, thanks to my work, a small corridor and thread can be laid through this bulwark, a view and insight into enormous human suffering often show up. This suffering, of course, has to do with mental suffering, which settles close to death. As if people – more often it is women, children and babies with whom I work – have to carry a basic fundamental lack of narcissistic care within and with them throughout their lives. Of course, what I call the "resistance bulwark" applies less to babies and children than to adults. This facilitates the corresponding psychoanalytical work.

The narcissistic attention should, according to the Quran, be directed in older children and adults – psychoanalytically speaking – towards God, towards Mohammed the Prophet or towards the man (father). This on the one hand. On the other hand, the mothers, due to their large number of children and often at the same time their responsibility for the family's daily bread, are completely overburdened practically 24 hours a day. They themselves hardly receive any narcissistic attention, especially none from their marriage, forged by their own parents (their father), and are thus hardly in a position to give their children sufficient narcissistic attention. On the contrary, a great deal is demanded of children from an early age, especially of girls, since boys are more socially desirable and respected. If at all, children find a minimum of narcissistic attention from their siblings, from aunts who have few or no children of their own or from grandmothers. The older siblings also give the younger ones a certain amount of attention, and the gratitude of the younger ones in turn can retroactively strengthen the narcissism of the older ones a little.

6   *Psychoanalytic work in East African cities*

In my psychoanalytic work, the narcissistic attention, the narcissistic weight that I give to the patients and the child patients, the babies, in looking at them, in listening to them, in smelling them, in my fantasising about the patients and my reverie of them and, depending on the situation, also in slight physical contact (physical contacts are part of the social exchange in these ethnic groups; a counterpart, especially a sick counterpart, can hardly cope with their refusal), probably plays the most important role.

Vignettes

Now, for a better understanding of what I call religious-Islamic resistance, two vignettes from my clinical work in East Africa.

The following vignette shows – initially – Quranic resistance or resistance against a deeper therapeutic contact seemingly in favour of adherence to Islamic rules.

A young woman breathing "nothing"

Y is 15 years old, forcibly married by her father to a man about 25 years older. The other women in the hospital are around 60 years old – people in East Africa live fewer years than in Western Europe – and are often psychosomatically completely broken down, especially through drug use. Y, like all girls and young women, can change her image and social status thanks to her marriage to an (older) man. She is already a "woman" by definition, from and since her genital mutilation. Through her marriage to an older man, she becomes a woman with a man, or more precisely, a woman under the direction of a man. This guardianship is intended to encourage or induce the woman to live in accordance with the Quran, often by means of the threat of punishment.

In short psychotherapeutic conversations with Y, she always tells me that her husband is very good to her and she is silent about her father. Not to say anything critical or not positive about one's own father or husband is a statement that corresponds to the Quran and at the same time also enables self-protection, because of the reaction of the men, which is something I heard from many women of different ethnicities, for example Somali and Ifar, and from women from Ethiopia, Sudan and Eritrea.

Y returns to the clinic voluntarily this second time, at night, probably when she realised (this is my interpretation) that she needs protection. Perhaps from her husband? The clinic diagnoses her coming, at night, barefoot, without money, as psychotic behaviour. Psychoanalytically, I understand her action as a psycho-physical act that is probably appropriate to the circumstances, as a search for protection and self-protection in the form of an escape away from home. Y acts purposefully and in no way out of touch with reality. Her sole, independent entry into the hospital, neither ordered nor accompanied by her father or husband, is scandalous within the framework of the Quranic regulations. After all, being barefoot and without money is nothing unusual per se for a poor East African woman.

According to my diagnostic assessment, Y is not primarily psychotic but traumatised, which she tries to "process" by depressively and psychologically dissociating and by means of denial. The hospital's internal diagnosis is based, I think, on Islamic legislation for Muslim women: women are not supposed to think for themselves and not to distance themselves from their husband or even – alone – to flee from him.

In the first psychotherapeutic consultation Y answers my questions, such as what happened, how she feels, how her husband is, how she feels here in the hospital etc., all with the same words and gestures. She always says extremely quietly, as it were in a breath: "Nothing."

During the second conversation with Y, I again ask her various questions and her answer is still: "Nothing." It seems to me that apart from her shyness and shame towards and in the strange situation and towards me, there is a lot of denial, especially in upholding loyalty to the Islamic rules. A woman should not talk or complain about her married life or about her own painful experiences and thoughts. I maintain my interest in her and what has happened and am not deterred by the "nothing". Furthermore, my occupation and orientation towards her own insufficiently developed narcissism – hearing, seeing, smelling, fantasising, reverie – applies entirely to the young patient. Without pressuring her, I speak calmly to her now and then. In this way I also try to convey to her that she has scope for freedom and is not my self-object. And I hope that this becomes perceptible and tangible for her herself. I remain interested – in my countertransference, however, I see myself increasingly helpless and powerless – and gently ask this and that and explain to her that I think that what knocks us down, what makes us despair, helpless and sad, has roots in our own lives. I describe a little piece of psychoanalytic optics that might well question the Islamic law: everything comes and goes thanks to Allah. A bit as if believing people were self-objects of their God.

All of a sudden she mumbles very quietly, and as if it didn't concern her, that she gave birth to a dead baby six weeks ago. "That's bad and very, very sad," I say. "No," she says. She forgot about it, it's not bad at all. She doesn't know anything about it anymore. Me: *How could she not know anything more about it?* I think this and I say it to her. "I don't know," she answers. Now she breathes again, as in the first conversation, the very quiet "nothing" throughout. She is probably also in denial and dissociating. At the same time, the religious-cultural norms play their inhibiting role: Allah wanted it that way and therefore her misfortune (trauma or rather traumata) is right and not worth mentioning, so to speak. Her husband knows nothing about the stillbirth and neither does the clinic.

At the beginning of the third conversation, Y hardly seems more fear-free or relaxed. After she had whispered "nothing" many times, I carefully and gently mirrored her and described how she seemed to want nothing more in her life ("nothing") and asked her if there had ever been other times when she had felt happier and more fun, perhaps when she had sung or danced. Her face immediately became brighter and more open and she said: "Yes." And I asked: "When?" Before she got married, she used to sing or listen to music and dance at home, and she was happy then.

This new memory seems to have reawakened a vivid psychic part of the patient: she was once, before her marriage, happy and joyful.

The fourth time I see Y is during the drawing group. After Y discovers me at the central table, her facial expression changes and becomes bright. She sits down in the middle of the bench, at the centre of the table board, looks at me and begins to organise herself in a tidy and vivid way. She passes paper and pencils to the others and explains if fellow patients have not understood what I am telling them, with the help of a translator. She then begins to draw herself. As soon as something important or additional can be said or done, Y is now the one who initiates it. She seems completely awake, attentive and obviously sees herself as responsible for her fellow patients and supports them. I am amazed at the psychic change Y has undergone in the last few days. As if, due to our psychotherapeutic work, a change from a depressive, almost lifeless life, probably a feeling of being or becoming extinct, from a severe depressive passivity and dissociation to an awakened liveliness and at the same time a good ability to relate could unfold. According to André Green, a change from death narcissism to life narcissism becomes possible.

This change, I think, also has to do with the fact that the young woman Y has probably noticed that I am neither outwardly nor inwardly influenced by Quranic rules – without devaluing them towards her – and that I in turn do not prevent her emerging desire for independence and being alive, but bear with it and perhaps even support it. Now it is also possible to think that she, covered by the constant "nothing", has latently unfolded an idealising transference towards me, which interestingly frees her from her somewhat paranoid-schizoid view of the world and enables her to adopt a depressive position, a somewhat different view, as Melanie Klein describes it. She turns to her fellow patients. She wants them to enjoy participating in drawing together and to understand what it is all about. She becomes active and takes on a certain responsibility for herself and for her environment – also for me, by helping me to organise.

After this meeting at the drawing table made of rough wooden boards, I can't speak to Y any more. I fly back to Europe. The next time I return, I ask if anyone knows how Y is doing. Well, they tell me, she left the hospital right after I left. And, she has divorced her husband, moved out of the village and is doing well. Despite the divorce, she is apparently doing well. I reply, controversially from a Quranic point of view, but in line with my diagnostic optics: "I think she's fine, precisely because she's divorced." My Muslim interlocutor reacts to this statement with astonishment, as if it were incomprehensible. And somehow dangerous.

At the beginning of the talks with Y, I had already suspected that she was mentally in a bad state, mainly because of the negative conditions in her marriage, which was a forced marriage. But the patient, as mentioned, did not utter a negative word about the state of her marriage or about her husband. She adhered to the rules of the Quran in this.[1]

And as someone who thinks and works psychoanalytically, I am sometimes in a not entirely harmless contradiction to the current Islamic religious culture.[2]

Sometimes it looks as if, because of the Quranic norms or the normative idea that God is in control of everything and that what he does and allows to happen is OK, there is actually nothing left for the individual that can still be changed on his or her own. And this naturally leads to a certain lethargy and passivity.[3] Not infrequently I find myself in situations where I am amazed or shocked that no help is forthcoming. Probably the often extremely meagre, daunting (to a European eye) and unendurable, all too deprived and depressing living conditions and human existence have a negative effect on empathic encounters with other people. The view of patients or generally needy people in some East African cities seems to be a partly blunted and not very empathetic one. Perhaps it was different in earlier times. The bleak situation in which the respective country finds itself, combined with the usually quite hopeless situation of the babies and children of the overburdened and genitally mutilated mothers – mostly affecting people of the lower and middle classes – and of course many other people in the big Black continent, makes hopelessness a contagious disease, as it were. And of course, the promises of the Islamic religion can bring a certain, mainly illusory, relief. I have to be careful not to become too infected by this more or less general hopelessness. It seems to me that a little infection of myself by all the hopelessness I encounter is unavoidable.

A lost woman forgotten in her rusted bed

To illustrate what I mean by "limited empathy", I present the following clinical vignette about Ms A.

A person in charge at the psychiatric hospital asks me to go to a patient who does not speak. He could not work for her.[4] In retrospect, it turns out that the patient had already been in the psychiatric hospital for three to four months, without anyone having made more intensive efforts to help her. She was fed and at night saw the other patients who lay down in their iron beds near her to sleep. Ms A was left to wither away, so to speak. A young woman shows me the way to her and then stays by my side. I can't see her in the old, dark corridor, which is dilapidated with cracks in the walls, but mainly because she is completely covered and lies with her head under the dirty bedclothes. In addition, an intense and very unpleasant smell of urine and faeces emanates from the bed. If I want to make contact with Ms A, I have to endure it. It is the smell that envelops her and so she can seek and

10 *Psychoanalytic work in East African cities*

find some security in her own smell. This on the one hand. On the other hand, this extremely unpleasant smell also concentrates her fear of other people. On the way, she can in a more or less inconscient way control or slow down the intrusion of others. Embedded in the strong smell is also her resistance, her defence. She doesn't seem to want anything more. I say her name. Nothing comes back and nothing stirs. It stinks terribly. (Later I see that the sheet metal that lies on the iron frame as a mattress base has already rusted through because too much urine seeped through the plastic mattress on it and remained pooled there.) I say something to the patient, a few words translated into Swahili. She does not respond. I continue to concentrate on her, so I don't allow myself to be pushed away, and from then on I say nothing but very calmly, rhythmically and melodiously her name.[5] I repeat it again and again. Maybe 20 times, whereby my speech melody is probably more important than the letters of her name. Very slowly, in slow motion, so to speak, she pushes the blanket a little away from her face and tries, also very slowly, to open one eye after the other. And now she looks at me silently out of strikingly large, needy, pleading children's eyes. I will need this ritual, namely repeating her name melodiously, more often to get in touch with her. For quite a while I don't know if she can speak at all. Finally, she begins to slur some words, as it were, in response to some questions I ask her, and I try to understand. What I hear above all is the word abandoned and the name of her birthplace, which is quite far away. She speaks a bit of English and that means she must have attended school, so she is somewhat educated and literate. I try to explain to her that it would be good if she got out of bed and had a shower, and that the young woman will help with that. When she goes to the showers, which can hardly be called showers in the European sense, I see that she walks with one leg or foot only on the tip of her foot. She is disabled and can only limp with difficulty. From now on, it is possible for me to touch her with my chanting of her name, my presence, my hearing her and seeing her, smelling her, and seduce her a little in the direction of narcissism of life, to a certain liveliness, so that now and then she leaves the bed and goes outside with the other patients. And she probably waits to see if I will come there. She remains an outsider in the hospital environment and is hardly able to make contact with others. The others are not kind to her; they try to make fun of her. She probably remains in a certain childlike dependence on me. And I cannot fulfil her many and great wishes and expectations.

It is not that this patient was mute or mutistic, but that no language was found that touched her sufficiently. And this language was not found mainly because of what I just mentioned: the lost empathy. Perhaps it was because of thoughts others could have had like nobody would ever come near to her, nobody would ever look for her as a invalid, nobody loves her, that A, without my attempts at contact, slowly perished in her tin pot. Now, when I come back from Europe, she is more withdrawn again, lives mainly in bed again and then, when she sees me, starts to get up again or even go outside.

The last time I went to see her especially, I could not find her. I asked around and was told that they had never had a patient like this. I answered, "Sure, you have had this patient; she walked like this," and I showed how the invalid patient had used her right foot. "Oh," they said. "Yes, she was here, but died in her bed, when we had an epidemic. We thought she was being attended to and we did not look after her intensively."

This idea that a special language is needed to reach a person and that everyone can only be touched and interested in this way is missing in many public and private medical and care institutions, hospitals and homes. And perhaps this also has to do with the fact that the helpers and people in charge, who are often also in need, say to themselves: I already have too much work; if God does not look and does not intervene, there is nothing I can do.

Notes

1 There are also matrilineally structured ethnic groups in some East African countries, where of course different marriage rules apply.
2 This has been observed with interest not only in some of my previous East African places of work.
3 When I talk to Muslims about this point in more detail, many emphasise that this formulation is not correct. God helps above all when people live according to God's standards. Efforts are also required of the believer.
4 For a long time, this case had been solely about finding out where the patient's parents or family were in order to deport Ms. A there. The "integration" into the family of origin is usually regarded as more important than an attempt to understand the individual suffering of a patient.
5 I have developed and used the melodious, rhythmic, repeated pronunciation of the name in my work with babies and orphans and have experienced that this can create a human exchange.

2 Psychoanalytic fieldwork in East African cities

In some East African countries, where I have been working for about nine years, during short stays in the country, the cultures of different ethnic groups blur and mix.[1] From this point of view, it is not possible for me to approach or describe my work with an ethnological view that is essentially focused on a single ethnic group.[2]

The people of these East African multi-ethnic societies willy-nilly live together to guarantee their meagre survival. The current mix of ethnicities has a lot to do with the societies' political situations. I am referring mainly to refugees from other ethnicities and cultures. But also information from Western African countries[3] or about European and possibly American cultural behaviour changes over time the social and ethno-cultural urban situation of the country in which ethnically different or even oppositely oriented people take refuge. This is of course especially true for smaller countries, because there is too little space to live at a distance from others. Nevertheless, the dwellings are often designed in such a way that ethnic groups "conquer" their own neighbourhoods or districts and occupy them as best they can.

Some older locals experience themselves as people who live in parallel worlds: the "old world" with all the ethno-cultural conditions that are associated with it, and in and with which they grew up, and precisely next to it exists the other world.[4]

The older generation wants to preserve what has come down through the ages, as it seems to them to be sacred; from our European perspective, on the other hand, the same ritual that is so central to certain African ethnic groups can be seen as terribly brutal and destructive. Such rituals include East African circumcision or mutilation rituals of the female genitals (Saegesser 2014) and in certain ethnic groups also the mutilation of the female secondary sexual characteristics, the breasts. The mothers there bind their daughters' breasts, as soon as they become a little visible, with very tightly pulled cloths wound around the chest. Culturally, these acts, like genital mutilation, make a girl a woman by the African definition. They are therefore in the service of becoming a woman in a positive sense.[5]

DOI: 10.4324/9781003451587-2

Similar norms apply to circumcision of young boys or "adolescent" young men.[6] The time at which this happens in the life of a male baby or young and adolescent man varies depending on the African country and its respective important prevailing ethno-cultural rituals. In southern Ethiopia, a ritual existed and may still exist for the acceptance and incorporation of a younger man into the community of child-producing men: he is only accepted into the community after he has cut off the testicles of an old man from his ethnic group. This is what Paul Parin (1985) writes in his book *Too Many Devils in the Land*.

In most of the East African countries I worked in, I heard and saw how younger people are and are supposed to be completely respectful and even submissive towards their elders – mainly the older men (in some parts of Ethiopia, for example in the capital, parents are addressed with a formal mode of address) – and have to follow their instructions without fail.

This concerns the younger male generation and at the same time women, whatever their age. Women are also ruled over by brothers of the same age, or husbands, or the oldest and older men, who see themselves bound together as a council of elders, governing their lives, actions and deaths. Some – not all – of the younger generation, who not infrequently want to orient themselves to so-called westernised practices and no longer so much to their own cultural good, naturally try to evade this rule of absolute obedience to the fathers, and also the commandment of the primacy of family connections or family cohesion. In European terms, this applies above all to late adolescents.[7] For adolescent (in the European understanding) young women, it is almost impossible not to submit to the social rituals. Braving the hurdle to emancipate themselves is often de facto life-threatening for young women and women in general. I reported in Chapter 1 about a young woman, patient Y, who also took refuge in the psychiatric clinic under the huge pressure of this field of conflict.

If I understand the cultural rituals correctly, genital mutilation, which is cruelly inflicted on the girl from the age of four, sometimes of course earlier or a little later, is regarded as the beginning of female life as a woman par excellence, who is of course also a daughter. Her next stage of life – after being a child, i.e. after being mutilated – as a woman, which probably lasts her whole life, is, ethno-culturally speaking, marriage to a man, namely life as a wife. I wonder whether, in relation to the East African cities where I worked and work, one can even find a concept for the psychosexual development of the female child into a pubescent, adolescent younger and later female woman, all the way to becoming a wife and mother.

And something similar might apply to the psychosexual development of the boy who grows up in a city. Are there, for example, among his parents and relatives, models of his psychosexual development from a small boy to a young man to a family man? I think not. And I do not know.

14 *Psychoanalytic fieldwork in East African cities*

To emancipate themselves and get away from their family of origin, the late "adolescents" need money, among other things. And that is precisely what they do not have, except in the social upper class. At the same time, there are not enough opportunities. Even after completing an apprenticeship, only a few find a job. Sometimes more than 50% of young people are unemployed. This social problem naturally increases the chance that young men, especially in late "adolescence", can become criminals and often addicted to drugs at the same time.

And the boys are often left, almost as a survival strategy, with only the escape into crime and drug use. This can be seen and understood as an apparent way to get out of late adolescence. Perhaps this drug use is a kind of new ritual that makes boys – mainly men – believe they have strength and gives them the feeling of being adults and independent of their family of origin. Drug use naturally supports criminal activity and fantasies of greatness, which can actually be reduced more and more in the course of late adolescence in a favourable case. This drug use is sometimes extremely widespread. I saw this mainly where cities are located on a drug transit route and the drugs – especially cocaine, heroin and opium – can be bought up to 95% cheaper than in Europe, for example.[8]

The recollection of and recourse to the original ethnic culture often plays an important role again and somewhat unexpectedly when, for example, groups of "whites" want to offer help, possibly somewhat pushily. Then suddenly one's own original ethnic culture becomes important. It can be used, as it were, as a protective shield against anything new that "white" people from other cultures would like to bring, precisely in the sense of a perhaps extremely urgent relief action. Of course, this behaviour is quite understandable, especially because of the colonisation they have experienced.[9]

Today's national borders hardly correspond to the earlier, more organically developed national borders that took greater account of ethnicity. This constellation is probably one of the main reasons for the terrible war atrocities and genocides that we "witness" from afar, thanks to our Western means of information. Whereas the people who experience all this at first hand in the countries concerned do not have access to informative explanations of the events which we Western countries can make available to ourselves. Radio and television are usually considered political instruments and/or luxury goods.

What particularly interests and guides me in my psychoanalytic work in East African countries is made up of various aspects.

Certainly, something that is particularly stimulating for my individual work (I am not affiliated with any organisation) in East African cities and countries is the misery, the daily material, cultural and psychological misery, as well as the disregard for human rights, especially women's rights.

What has also guided me from the beginning is the question of whether I can use my psychoanalytic concepts: inner psychoanalytic frame, attempt to set up a more private intimate situation for two, listening closely, looking closely, mirroring etc., to interest and psychically touch people from completely different ethnic groups to which I do not belong.

Freud (1975/1919) writes: "For I have been able to help people with whom I had nothing in common in terms of race, education, social position and world view, without disturbing them in their idiosyncrasy" (p. 193). Well, this also applies to my work in East African countries.

I started my work in Muslim orphanages with babies and children, then I worked with male street children aged 5–22, then in a southern orphanage and school, later in neonatology and maternity for the poorest, next in a very rudimentary form of Islamic psychiatry, mainly for the lowest social class, and finally in a large hospital and its psychiatric dependency serving a large surrounding area.[10]

I work, as mentioned above, alternately in cities that do not allow for an exclusively ethnological perspective, as a creeping cultural change is evident in their reality. The ideology of the original ethnic cultures remains, parallel to the newer, somewhat changing society. I assume that Islamic culture is one that tends to oppose change and so-called progressive change. The dogma that is above all should not be changed. So, except within the conservative dogmatic Islamic framework, I do not work within a closed ethnic cultural sphere, as especially ethnologically oriented psychoanalysts have done and still do. I go where the patients are and not the other way round, as this would mainly correspond to the European psychoanalytic working culture.

I am often asked: How do you communicate with children, young people and adults without speaking their mother tongues? Well, what I spontaneously perceive, thanks to my occupation that supports the narcissism of the other person, which of course does not primarily focus on the deconstruction of psychological processes, immediately leads me on a first track, on a certain trail, later of course on an additional one, and then usually on another and another and another. It's a basic exchange, as Bion would say, between the container and what is placed in the container. And of course, within the framework of my psychoanalytic work, I try to perceive and go along and, if possible, let a connection happen between my unconscious and the unconscious of my East African patient. I assume that the structure of the unconscious, whether European or East African, is essentially the same: the unconscious is unconscious.

I try to perceive my counterpart, the patient, integrally, by which I mean: to take note of the verbal, gestural and physical, i.e. the scenic, such as the postures, movements, involuntary, uncontrolled sounds and smells of the counterpart. From that which becomes manifest, that shows itself, by which I can be captivated, I try, without communicating this naturally, to construct the latent and to see this to some extent and perhaps to understand it.

Next I describe my work with street boys.

Notes

1 In various chapters of my book I mention and describe again certain processes and contents of faith etc. which I have already described before. This is to emphasise the importance of the content and to keep open the possibility of reading individual chapters and understanding them sufficiently well.
2 My observation situation is different from that of Paul Parin (1985) and Parin et al. (1972).
3 However, television, especially foreign television, can only be received in a few households of the socially upper class because it would be too expensive.
4 You might think, "Yes, and that exists in more Western countries as well." The range of difference between the worst poverty and social misery, and the paradisiacal ideas of "Western life", is incomparably greater in East African cities.
5 I cannot go into detail here about other meanings of all these destructions – seen from a European perspective – of the female body. I mention just this one piece of information about female genital mutilation: it has nothing to do with Islam in the narrower sense, but was already used as a ritual beforehand, probably by the Egyptians.
6 The concept of adolescence does not resonate in East African urban areas. It is a European concept. I will come back to this later.
7 I am talking here about life in cities; in more rural areas, there are other rituals, especially for boys who – according to the European understanding – are in puberty.
8 There are East African countries that promote drug use, such as khat, up to the highest government circles, because the state makes a lot of money thanks to the taxation of khat.
9 When it comes to the concept of colonising, it is often forgotten that this form of domestication is not and was not first imported and practised, as it were, by foreign, non-coloured Western powers. In Sudan, for example, which was once much larger in area, wealthier urban dwellers colonised the physically much stronger mountain dwellers in prehistoric times, bringing them into the cities as slaves for themselves. And of course, Arabs, Persians and other peoples repeatedly tried to colonise the Black African lands and people.
10 Socially higher-ranking and financially well-off residents seek medical help in other countries, such as Arab countries, Turkey, and of course also in European countries in well-established clinics.

Bibliography

Freud, Sigmund (1919). *Paths of Psychoanalytic Therapy*. Study edition. Supplementary volume. Frankfurt am Main: Fischer, 1975.

Parin, Paul (1985). *Zu viele Teufel im Land. Aufzeichnungen eines Afrikareisenden.* Frankfurt am Main: Syndikat.

Parin, P., Morgenthaler, F. and Parin-Matthèy, G. (1972). *Die Weißen denken zuviel. Psychoanalytische Untersuchungen bei den Dogon in Westafrika*. München: Kindler Taschenbücher.

Saegesser, Barbara (2014). Psychoanalytische Arbeit mit BB's, Kleinkindern und Müttern in unterschiedlichen afrikanischen Ländern (Le travail psychanalytique avec les bébés, des petits enfants et des mères dans divers pays d'Afrique). *Schweizerische Gesellschaft für Psychoanalyse (SGPsa) Bulletin* No. 77 (Spring): 5–13.

3 Drop-in and home for street boys

The institution at which I am working for a short period (over Christmas) is a combined drop-in clinic and residential home. The policy there, which takes the form of strict rules and regulations, is to attempt to more or less eradicate "adolescent" behaviour, e.g. the kind of behaviour that manifests itself as acting as though the general rules of behaviour do not apply to one. It is a Christian-run facility, although nearly all of the "residents" have an Islamic background, as does most of the country's population.

These "street boys" have lived and are living something like a grand "adolescence", which involves a great deal of self-aggrandisement as omnipotent and which, in confrontations with another reality, an adult reality in the street and in the market, can express itself in what seem to be very strange forms of behaviour. There is certainly no way to entirely block out the actions, the haggling and hustling that go on in these huge, sprawling markets. Other, that is, than by retreating into the fantasy world in which good parents love their "wonderful boys". It seems to me that an important element in this confrontation with the reality of something that happens at the market is witnessing the reality that adults' behaviour towards one another is not always "good" – as children usually wish it were – seeing that they often cheat, swindle, threaten or covertly mistreat one another, particularly in life on the street or at one of these vast markets. As in most African countries, these markets are normally outdoors and are places where one can trade or shop for almost any kind of goods. The markets tend to be used mainly by people of lower social status and people who are poor, including the very poorest of the poor. And this life on the streets is probably one that demands that young people have a lot of skills, i.e. survival strategies.

The psyche of the young men is overburdened, their development has more or less come to a standstill, or rather, any development that does take place is concentrated on certain skills and abilities, for instance group solidarity and cohesion in a crisis, hiding, running away, lying, stealing, tricking people, presenting and prostituting oneself and, ultimately, the ability to survive amidst all the chaos.

DOI: 10.4324/9781003451587-3

18 *Drop-in and home for street boys*

This probably happens more through imitation than identification. Of course, this can also give rise to an identification with deceased or absent parents. This identification is with parents, who, though idealised, were not or are not actually concerned about their child, which is to say, with parents who are or were not sufficiently containing and responsible and from whom the child can hardly learn how to take care of themselves in a reasonably humane fashion. In the case of children orphaned at an early age, they probably did not spend enough time with their "real parents" to establish a basis for an identification with a lively and self-preserving life. I believe that this results in a kind of as-if maturity and as-if identity, a premature ego-strength. The boys and young men are forced into a psychophysical maturity that comes too early, the ego develops too early and too hastily, and often involves an affectation of omnipotent external behaviour that in no way reflects the person's internal psychological realities. In order to survive, the younger and older "adolescents" also need a great deal of intelligence or cleverness. The life of a child on the street or in the vast, labyrinthine markets requires enormous vigilance, like that required of an adult, but more so. The street boys must fight to survive every hour of every day and every night, and this struggle is more extreme, more brutal than that of most adults in the country. The younger boys and older boys approaching manhood hide or gather in groups, whose shelter leaves them less exposed in their activities. Or they steal and let themselves be sexually exploited, usually by adult men (traders, merchants, the younger among the elders etc.).

The young boys and the older "adolescents" often offer their sexual "skills", selling sexual services which, by enabling them to feel important and desirable in the eyes of these adults, as they were not in the eyes of their parents, can occasionally even give them a feeling that nourishes their narcissism. They allow themselves to be sexually abused and exploited without being aware that they are doing so. The boys do not regard this sexual and psychological exploitation as something that is only bad and that has to be put up with, but also as a means of survival for them and, as I said, it can also serve to provide food, though food of a toxic kind, for their undernourished narcissism. Moreover, the streets and the markets themselves are imbued with quasi-fantasised parental qualities. Any street might be a kind of "Hotel Mama" and might provide more, or something different, than was or is provided by their biological mother. It is a self-service set-up where one can obtain (almost) anything, as long as one is sufficiently clever in going about it.

Thus, my assumption is that intersubjective interactions of sufficiently good quality were too infrequent or entirely absent from very early on in the life of these boys. The boys' ability to mentalise was unable to develop properly. The street boys are victims of their family situations and local conditions, although they often go for long periods of time without seeing themselves as victims, as doing so might make it even more difficult

Drop-in and home for street boys 19

for them to survive. The psyche attempts to repress or split off this being exposed/abandoned through fantasies of omnipotence, and other functions. For instance, a boy may see himself as one of the "chosen few", people who "seemingly" stand above certain circumstances.

The street boys with whom I worked in the home were essentially given no opportunity to gain a better understanding of their own actions or of themselves. The managers of the home were intent on drilling them into form, so to speak; they were to leave their past lives behind and begin to live and act in accordance with societal norms. Among those running the home, perhaps the strongest motivation for helping these children was an unqualified desire to "forge" these boys into Christians. Which in itself actually constituted another abuse, another rape of the "adolescents" and "late adolescents", i.e. boys on the cusp of adulthood.

The basic social pattern of people's behaviour towards the boys repeats itself: they are exploited to further the agenda of their exploiters, in this case, for Christian aims and purposes. And being subjected to this exploitation without having been asked, in order to satisfy someone else's, i.e. the perpetrators', need to feel powerful – in all of the varied nuances that can be found – is precisely what they have already been experiencing for many years. The boys had to work towards their own survival by relying on their own wits and through exploitation, primarily sexual exploitation, or rather by allowing themselves to be exploited. The situation inside the home is not that different in many respects. There, they are supposed to be remade into "objects" pleasing to the people who run the home, thereby enabling these same people to accord themselves Christian narcissistic importance. Despite all these attempts on the part of management to "domesticate" the home's residents and, in a sense, to misuse them for their own purposes (by converting them to Christianity, for instance), the children continue to manifest some of the psychological and physical traits they developed in their earlier life on the street. Not all of these can be "erased". Younger residents are sometimes brutally sexually abused by the older boys. This is not about sexual experimentation, which would be age appropriate. It is about exercising power. The acts themselves are severely harmful and destructive and yet are, whenever possible, ignored or swept under the carpet by those running the home. What a boy has passively experienced is activated and reversed and "applied" on another resident, usually a younger one, of course. And naturally, there is much kept secret that continues to be important for the younger and older street boys, such as stealing, lying, being cleverer than those around them etc.

I attempt to use drawing as a means for communication with these street boys, the vast majority of whom were orphaned at an early age or have no more contact with their parents. The head of the home had expected something quite different: a more vigorous, authoritarian approach. I had to make considerable use of my powers of persuasion to present my project

20 *Drop-in and home for street boys*

in a light enabling it to be, if not welcome, at least tolerated, and refusing to deviate from my own ideas about it demanded no small degree of stubbornness on my part.

I chose the activity of drawing with pencils and with a predefined subject – specifically, their parents and/or siblings – as the "pedal point" underpinning the entire psychotherapeutic encounter. This choice was shaped by language considerations (my Arabic skills are extremely rudimentary, and the boys spoke only rudimentary English). I decided against an unstructured form of drawing, because I was particularly interested in the relationship with the parents, who, for whatever reasons, were not present or not available to the boys. I was interested in seeing how they would react emotionally to and during the assignment. Could they remember a familial environment? Could I learn something about their inner parents, their representations of parents?

Even playing Winnicott's squiggle game with the home residents is very difficult to arrange in this environment. The idea of playful drawing together is too complicated to explain under the conditions there. Moreover, the boys' access to the free play of thoughts and imagination seemed somewhat limited. In the squiggle game, freedom is key: freedom in perceiving the other person's squiggle and in using one's imagination to make something out of it. It is about subjective freedoms of the individual and about freedom in (dream) thinking and responding. It seems likely that the unduly harsh life and dogmatised cultural rules governing life in the home are factors contributing to a strong impediment against their ability to mentalise and fantasise within a circumscribed context. I also wonder if the Islamic culture contributes to making free thinking and creating more difficult or even prevents it entirely. The template, the rule may be more important than the creativity of the subject in this cultural group.

I gave the same assignment to all of the home's residents, or rather, to each of the home's residents who dared to have something to do with me, to sit with me without knowing what would happen: to draw their parents and then their siblings as well.

I found a quieter corner that was not totally exposed – outside, in front of the common rooms – where I could "talk" to the boys. Partly this took place using the language of actions, i.e. using the props to hand, and partly with the help of rudimentary translations.

The first resident I worked with was assigned to me by the team that ran the home. He was chosen because he could speak a little English. His behaviour towards me was very timid, fearful. He spoke at such a low volume that it was almost as though he were speaking only to himself. This seemed to arouse the curiosity of other home residents and the head of the home immediately. I had barely begun to communicate with him in the way I described when a group of young spectators began to gather a certain distance away from us. The head of the home, who liked to interfere, suddenly came up with coloured pens for me – I was working with pencils. But this, very quickly awakened, interest, which seemed to dampen the boys' fear of the "unknown", probably also had to do with the survival training provided by the streets. Soon, they were all pushing forward; they all wanted to "have" some too, and they wanted it right away. Fortunately, they were not yet so resigned or so depressive that they did not want to take part. An encounter of a kind unknown to them triggered their interest immediately. Their perception, from a distance, of the encounter as a moving and calming one probably played a role here. To apply Bion's (2023) model, I can see and understand this as the transmission of positive containing.

This interest of mine, exclusively focused on the individual present, was immediately absorbed, in a positive sense, as in the sense of narcissistic sustenance. The boys did not develop any fears, or not obviously anyway – at most a bit of scepticism here and there. I asked them to use a pencil to draw their parents and/or siblings. An interesting observation here is that externally, they all chose to go about it in the same way: first sketching the outline of human figures, with an extremely light touch and in a fragile manner. All of them did this in exactly the same way. It seems likely that they had been told that they should draw this way in the home. There was a noticeable brittleness and self-consciousness associated with the way they expressed themselves with this strictly controlled pressure in their strokes. Next, the boys drew over the same lines, pushing down hard, in enormous, stiff, almost completely uniform strokes. Symbolically, the gentle was covered by the omnipotent, the liveliness with stiffness. This, then, was the external framework, the drawing technique.

And their content? For the most part, the figures in the drawing were completely stylised and stiff. This may have had to do with the rendering externally (onto paper) of the internally represented parents. Idealised, and above all robot-like, depictions of parents or of parents and siblings. In all of the street boys' pictures, one could see the image of the absent and thus the idealised. As I interpreted this (for myself alone, of course: naturally, I could not simply share my thoughts with the boys straight out) – the boys experienced and introjected their parents as persons with whom practically no intersubjective exchange could take place.

The absence of the parents was in most cases due to their death (often of AIDS). Moreover, one thinks, of course, of parents or (as was often the case) single mothers who were depressive, completely overburdened, both internally and externally, with nerves worn raw (due to their extremely precarious situations). Parents who had or sought next to no contact with their children. The latter, now "hard-nosed adolescents", seemed to have forgotten why they had been torn from or run away from their homes and developed a life of their own, a lifestyle of their own, and begun to live it. They had split off one part of their biography. I believe the drawings of the parents would have been a bit livelier if this were an instance of repression.

22 *Drop-in and home for street boys*

I am not sure whether the phrase "torn from" accurately describes what happened. Perhaps the "home" was more of a kind of place to be, one which did not necessarily provide the child with any form of protection. An African "home" is not at all comparable with the average European home. The experience of younger and older children, usually as one of many siblings (the average is around ten), is often that they can stay out, away from home, without anyone in their family ever asking where they were or have been. They may leave home early in the hope of finding and leading a better life without parents or other family members. Or they leave because their parents are dead. Sometimes, in some cultural environments, the parents send their children away, to relatives perhaps, because they now have younger children and want to take care of them.

Now I will return to the questions I asked above, which interested and still do interest me, and try to answer them. Here, again: How did the boys react emotionally to and during the assignment?

Only with difficulty could I make out signs of emotion directly in their faces or gestures. Their expressions seemed full of expectation, more satisfied than not, concentrated and, overall, a bit mask-like. Where the boys differed was in the way they applied themselves to the drawing. Some of them lowered their heads and began to draw right away. No time for emotion here, they signalled, or so I understood this to mean. Others hesitated, sending questioning looks my way. They could not decide how they wanted to place the figures within the space on the paper. They seemed ill at ease, almost overwhelmed and anxious.

Could the boys remember a familial environment?

It is difficult to say. Some of them seemed to, for their drawings seemed a bit more alive than those of the others and showed details, a revolver or booted feet, for instance. These details would accord, of course, with "late adolescent" fantasies about the idealised, absent, strong-as-an-ox father. In reality, there were no boots like this to be had in this country. The fantasised father had probably been sent to the "rich paradise" abroad. The fathers came across as weightier than the mothers in these pictures. The latter were often depicted with very large breasts that were emphasised. I could associate this with a desire for mother's milk / to suckle at the breast. Also with the fantasy of the mother as the most beautiful of all or – and this is not at all unlikely – the possibility that she was a very erotic figure in reality, perhaps a prostitute.

Could I learn something about their representations of parents?

I saw predominantly idealised, stiff, robot-like human figures in the drawings of the street boys, irrespective of the individual drawer's age. In many of the pictures, the figures were not really standing on the ground. They tended to be hanging somewhere in the air in the space of the paper. The symbolism of this might be understood as indicating not quite perceived or not truly present parents, or parents who do not convey the sense of safe ground.

Regarding the drawing technique:

The drawings were begun in an overly cautious and fragile manner with thin, powerless, tentative little strokes, after which all of these faint, more gentle strokes were covered and at the same time crushed by stiff, lifeless strokes applied with disproportionately heavy pressure. This might have been about defending against gentleness, which one would need to view and understand with reference to the drawer's age; perhaps this could also be an ethno-cultural learned defence. From a psychoanalytic perspective, it may have been a denial of one's own pain or perhaps also of the pain that the parents had experienced in the presence of their small children. I ran into this latter situation quite often. Even with very young children who lived in the same room with parents dying of AIDS, right up until their actual death.

Bibliography

Bion, W. (2023). *Learning from Experience*. London: Karnac Books.

Charlier, M. (2006). Geschlechtsspezifische Entwicklung in patriarchalisch-islamischen Gesellschaften und deren Auswirkung auf den Migrationsprozess. *Psyche – Zeitschrift für Psychoanalyse* 60(2): 97–117.

Freud, S. (1919). *Wege der psychoanalytischen Therapie*. Studienausgabe, suppl. vol. Frankfurt am Main: Fischer, 1982.

Hirsi Ali, A. (2015). *Reformiert euch! Warum der Islam sich ändern muss*. München: Albrecht Knaus Verlag.

Parin, Paul (1985). *Zu viele Teufel im Land. Aufzeichnungen eines Afrikareisenden*. Frankfurt am Main: Syndikat.

Parin, P., Morgenthaler, F. and Parin-Matthèy, G. (1972). *Die Weißen denken zuviel. Psychoanalytische Untersuchungen in Westafrika*. München: Kindler Taschenbücher.

Pradelles de Latour, Ch.-H. (1997). *Le crâne qui parle*. Deuxième édition de Ethnopsychanalyse en pays bamiléké. Paris: EPEL.

Pradelles de Latour, Ch.-H. (2014). *La dette symbolique. Thérapies traditionnelles et psychanalyse*. Paris: EPEL.

Racamier, Paul-Claude (1993). *Le psychanalyste sans divan. La psychanalyse et les institutions de soins psychiatriques*. Bibliothèque Scientifique Payot. Paris: Payot.

Saegesser, Barbara (2014). Psychoanalytische Arbeit mit BB's, Kleinkindern und Müttern in unterschiedlichen afrikanischen Ländern (Le travail psychanalytique avec les bébés, des petits enfants et des mères dans divers pays d'Afrique). *Schweizerische Gesellschaft für Psychoanalyse (SGPsa) Bulletin* No. 77 (Spring): 5–13.

Wohlfahrt, E. and Özbek, T. (2006). Eine ethnopsychoanalytische Kasuistik über das Phänomen der Besessenheit. *Psyche – Zeitschrift für Psychoanalyse* 60(2): 118–130.

4 Parenthood in East African cities

Psychoanalytic work with mothers, surrogate mothers, fathers and orphans[1]

Parenthood – biological, legal and social – as a Western European model of responsible interaction between a usually adult opposite-sex couple and mostly their own biological children, cannot have meaning in the East African cities I know, not in a "European" sense.[2] The predominant, legal-religious aspect of parenthood in East African countries usually gives all weight and power to fatherhood, both theoretically-culturally and in everyday action, in commanding, condemning, even killing a biological child or its biological mother. Fatherhood is fulfilled largely through the attribution and exercise of power.

The Quran demands respect and gratitude from one's own children towards their parents. Based on my experience, I assume that in practice, in everyday life, this religiously demanded respect actually takes the form of enormous fear, which is directed at the powerful father, much less at the mother. The father often leads a life next to his family and, to a certain extent, as though he were above them. As a man endowed with religious and cultural power according to the Quran, he cannot be given any "burdens", such as actually caring for and looking after his children. He is the (at least ascribed) biological father and thus, according to the Quran, he has the right to decide on the life or death of his family members. He has a financial duty to his family, but not a paternal duty to care for them. Seen in this light, fatherhood seems to be primarily a theoretical Quranic dictum that is based on the ascribed biological fatherhood, and not on a caring, everyday practical fatherhood that is present for the child. Nor in a desired joint, more or less symmetrical action of father and mother with their common children. The competence and power of disposal attributed to the father in his fatherhood are independent of what the father does for his offspring in his everyday life, except (but not always) for financial matters.

The form of theoretical, overly powerful fatherhood that has just been described and circumscribed diverges somewhat from the European

DOI: 10.4324/9781003451587-4

picture.[3] In this respect, it seems more sensible and appropriate, if at all, to speak of asymmetrical parenthood or to examine fatherhood and motherhood as separate models.

It looks to me as if implicitly, in social thinking and action, an impulse-giving idea, actually a desire of being practical, helping, protecting one's own and also the other children's partial parenthood in the form of a real existing motherhood, shows itself. The model of "parenthood" as a description of a form of partnership care for one's own children seems, for various reasons, not to be appropriate to describe the diverse way in which human family, predominantly maternal, action is exercised in East African regions. The father and mother of the children here[4] stand in extremely different roles. The father is theoretically, namely religious-culturally, thus legally[5] and ethnically, the unrestricted and untouchable dominant figure of his family.

In this respect, it seems more appropriate and meaningful to speak not of a model of parenthood but of theoretical outstanding fatherhood and practical outstanding motherhood.

The woman, the mother, or women and mothers and, of course, also girls, have a legally, i.e. religious-culturally, and ethnically quite inferior position. She has no say in anything and can – from a Western European point of view – be regarded and treated like a serf. Theoretically, the man determines everything, rules over everything. He is rightfully an absolute ruler.

In everyday life, however, the woman, the mother, usually bears the entire responsibility for her own life and the life and survival of her children, and sometimes also of her husband.[6] She is not only the one who gives birth to the children, but also the one who – sometimes unsuccessfully – tries to look after the children and who often also provides the daily bread. The most important parent in the family is the wife and mother, who is completely devalued by the Quran, completely subordinate to and at the mercy of her husband. As a rule, she takes over the active care for survival.

In the difficult, unbelievably difficult everyday life with the children and when it comes to the acquisition of daily food, many East African women, predominantly of the social lower and middle classes, stand alone. They give themselves the responsibility for their own survival and that of their families or, to put it another way, they inevitably have to take on "parenthood" for the existence of all those who depend on them. The wife looks after the children, and not infrequently there are around 15 children; she takes care of earning the money; and, if possible, she ensures the cohesion of the extended family. In some ethnic groups, a larger number of children promises the respective mother a higher social prestige, a better reputation. This can lead women to want to become pregnant again and again and to bear children, although they are virtually alone in the practical obligation of caring for them and there are no money and no food per se. Of course,

26 *Parenthood in East African cities*

these birth mothers are by no means happy expectant mothers but often completely overworked and exhausted and in many cases, at least latently, hopeless women for whom every new child means a great additional burden. And it is conceivable that the narcissism of the man also plays a role in the high number of children, if he himself, with his large flock of children, wants to show how fertile he is. This is likely to be particularly important in those ethnic groups where very young women, e.g. 15-year-olds, are married to much older men, e.g. 60-year-olds. I encountered such couple constellations mainly among Somali female patients.

A word about what I call theoretical fatherhood. Fathers are practically always absent from their families and hardly take care of them. Not even when their wives are at work or in hospital giving birth. If it is quite impossible for the mothers, then grandmothers, if they are still alive, or an aunt or another female relative, take care of the children. In the hospital, the patients always tell me that their husband is looking after the children during their current hospital stay and that he is very kind. The staff, on the other hand, sort of enlighten me and say: that's not true, they're lying. The men don't help their wives at all.

In many places I encounter this great shyness, actually ashamedness, to describe what is really going on. The vast majority of men or fathers, especially young fathers, in the East African areas where I work are unemployed or day labourers. It is not uncommon for them to use the money they have earned themselves for their personal drug consumption (often khat), leaving no money for their families. Shameful concealment or lying by wives, e.g. when it comes to blatant neglect by the husband, is mainly based on the fear of losing the husband through divorce if she reports unpleasant things about him. And a woman absolutely needs a husband in order to be socially integrated. Alone, as a divorced woman she is considered inferior. And a single woman, from a certain young age, is also considered inferior.

An unmarried woman cannot "be" a family with her child or children in some, not all, East African countries. She is denied parenthood. Often, if she remains unmarried, she is expelled from the society or ethnic group.

A single woman may throw away her newborn child, which reveals that she had sex out of wedlock (often in the form of rape), in order not to be expelled from society. Wives – not only from the lower classes – hardly dare to get divorced for the reasons mentioned above, and if they do try, they suffer serious consequences. They may be socially isolated and tend to be religiously outcast. Husbands are divorced at their request without having to give particularly good reasons. Currently, lower- and middle-class husbands get divorced in order to marry a young woman. The right serves the patriarch.

In some East African cultures and ethnic groups, it is not the young but the elderly and old men who are the most important members of the ethnic group. These highly respected councils of the elderly – exclusively men – call the shots. For men, old age per se can mean a great increase in prestige in many of these countries. The women, on the other hand, especially the older women, are 100% involved in caring for their children and grandchildren and not infrequently their nieces and nephews, and at the same time, whenever possible, they try to earn or "find" a little money. Grandmothers who are still alive stand in to take care of the children because of the high death rate and the gainful employment of younger women. The mothers sell homemade baked goods, clean for richer people, in some countries they work in construction and rarely, because they are forbidden from doing so and severely punished if caught, they prostitute themselves etc.

It seems to me that the division of parenthood into honour and power on the one side, the male side, and duty and burden on the other, the female side, which has now been drawn and described several times, hardly corresponds to the current Western European model of parenthood. In this context, it is probably also significant that data that belong to and help organise a Western European family structure, such as important life dates, are not known or not reliably known in certain East African countries because they have often not been considered worth mentioning and remembering until now.[7] In some regions, many citizens, even from the upper social class, do not know their birthday and, of course, also the birth dates of their parents and siblings as well as other life-specific data. Mostly, it is the mothers who know the birth dates of their children, for example. And understandably, because of the large number of their children, not always. The East African fields near the Sahel are often desert-like, unlike those in West Africa, for example. Farming is practically impossible. Here and there, in the rural regions or the suburbs, families or rather heads of families keep one or two chickens, maybe a small goat. In principle, I could not and cannot really understand what the people here live on, or better still, how they keep themselves alive. Many go hungry and starve, many have to look from day to day if they can find something small to eat. They find comfort for all the terrible, barely liveable hardship of their lives in religion. They say to themselves: Allah has willed it this way and insofar it is also right. Everything is in his power. He knows what he is doing.

My optics are limited, of course. And the statements about what "actually" happens are often somewhat veiled to me. I refer to all that I have seen and heard in different cultures and ethnic groups. I learn cultural realities indirectly or more directly from the behaviour and conversations of and with pregnant women, mothers, aunts, midwives, doctors, nurses and now and then husbands in the environment of orphanages, hospitals, psychiatric wards and friendships.

In everything I am told in conversation, the concealment of the factual is quite common. I think it has to do with the almost unattainable moral Quranic guidelines and the difference between them and real-life actions. To deviate from the precepts is bad and actually evil, and makes a person

28 *Parenthood in East African cities*

a bad believer. And so a conflict of shame arises that obscures some statements. Moreover, people here are ashamed of themselves, especially towards non-coloured people, because they think the white ones know and can do everything better. This also happens to me. And I always realise only after hearing different opinions on a matter that some things remain very unclear. Certainly, this veiling talk and action not only apply to me, "the white person",[8] but also to neighbours and friends, which can be part of human behaviour in general.

What is manifestly shown, as often and everywhere, does not actually correspond to what is latent. This concealment is also an attempt to not look too bad, too sinful, before one's own eye – the ego ideal – before the eye of others, but above all before the eye of God. Understandably, people want to make the lack they feel as such as little visible as possible. In my work, this problem led to some institutions fearing that I would see too closely what is actually at hand, namely that I would come across the additional more or less hidden misery. And people from outside the continent, even if they bring real support, are not readily welcome, especially in the long run – which hinders the possibility of gaining insight.

The main configurations that distinguish East African parenthood, i.e. motherhood, from Western European parenthood could be described as follows.

Parenthood in East African countries does not per se consist of a man and a woman or a same-sex couple. And in principle, in East African Islamic cities and regions, it never consists of a same-sex couple. The family consists of one man and potentially many wives; the Quran allows up to four wives, provided the man has enough money to support his many wives. All the children of these different wives who are children of the same father are considered siblings. The concept/notion of a stepmother or stepsiblings is practically non-existent. Paternity determines the family. Motherhood is secondary.[9]

The father remains determinant or co-determinant for life, also over the life and death of his daughter. He is potentially even more empowered to make decisions and exercise power than the husband of his daughter. The latter cannot, even in emergency situations, decide for herself or about herself. In the hospital I was often present when a woman in labour, in a situation that was extremely critical for her life, was unable to agree to a caesarean section herself. Her husband or her father had to decide. A caesarean section is forbidden, according to the Quranic rules, because it is sinful. The woman giving birth, who stands between life and death, cannot decide on the further course of the birth situation, and no doctor can or should do so either. This right belongs to the husband or father alone. If neither husband nor father can be reached in this extremely life-threatening situation for the mother and child, or if they are against a caesarean section and the doctor takes responsibility for the life-saving operation, it can happen that the husband really storms the hospital, rages loudly and in the

Parenthood in East African cities   29

process also threatens and terribly insults his wife, who barely survived thanks to the caesarean section.

The natural process of childbirth should apparently not be interrupted or disturbed, although it is precisely thanks to mutilating interventions in the female body, namely genital mutilation, that this can sometimes only be carried out with difficulty and with the acceptance of life-threatening risks, not really at all in accordance with "actual female nature".[10] Women in some of these countries are genitally mutilated, sometimes in the worst way, which bears the name la Pharaonica. The clitoris, the outer and inner labia are cut away and the genital opening is sewn together to a gap of about 2 cm. It is not uncommon for part of the bladder or another organ to be sewn in at the same time. All the tissue in the vagina and at its exit is scarred and hardened. This is another reason why women who give birth often have complications and suffer extreme pain. For the circumcised woman, childbirth is associated with the early traumatic situation of circumcision and tends to trigger re-traumatisation. In this area, too, the religious laws impose things hardly humanly acceptable on the Muslim woman, since all this takes place in an extremely precarious family situation. These are not mainly expectant and hopeful women who come to the hospital. They are those who do not give birth at home because of complications, and who at the same time have hardly any money for a first child or one additional to an already very large group of children. And some of the women did not want to get pregnant at all. However, according to the Quran, they have to surrender to everything their husband wants. But each child is an extra burden, because each child wants to eat, and they themselves, the mothers, have too little to eat. They are often extremely malnourished. Many newborns suffer from physical impairments. The mental maternal abstinence is added to the not really life-enabling somatic nutrition situation. Mental nourishment is missing for the mothers and thus also for the smallest and the little ones. The mothers are sometimes mentally hardly able to take care of their babies, because they themselves are in misery. I am not referring to the misery of postpartum depression, but to the everyday harrowing and despairing East African misery of survival. The newborns, who probably also during their time *in utero* are not particularly valued but have to be endured and carried along, as it were, suffer from a state of mental starvation. The mental side of a subject, according to the respective religious orientation, does not come into play. It does not exist, as it were, because there is only the believing human being subject to Allah. Man cannot subjectify himself, I mean, but is and should remain a self-object of Allah. He is a creature of Allah and Allah decides over man and is man's almighty point of reference in this world.

Now to some other impulses of East African parental, or rather maternal, thinking and action. Children of poor families with many children may be transplanted to a related family with fewer children or more money, or

30 *Parenthood in East African cities*

to a single childless aunt. The chosen kinship family does not necessarily live close to the family of origin. It is hardly possible for the child to see his or her biological family whenever he or she wants to. The passing on of one's own children makes a lot of sense, I am told, because it serves the cohesion of the larger family, which is also spread over different countries, i.e. the ethnic group or the clan. The fact that this transplantation could be bad for the child is not considered. The family structure is more important than the life of the individual child and the individual woman.[11] A parental, i.e. maternal, thought and the model of foster motherhood are clearly present and recognisable.

In certain regions, a large part of the parents' generation is missing. They have died of AIDS. Grandmothers or aunts take care of the orphans left behind, if possible. An orphaned child in Western European terms, however, does not exist in the Quran and accordingly not in many cities, since children who become parentless are theoretically immediately passed on to relatives. Orphanages are usually not immediately recognisable as such, because there are actually no orphans. In fact, there are many orphanages that are seldom called orphanages, but rather house X or house Y. It also happens that the orphanages are called orphanages. It also happens that the first lady of the country, i.e. the wife of the president, declares herself the mother of all parentless children. Accordingly, there are no orphans there, according to the Quran.

In these arrangements, a pronounced claim to motherhood is again clearly implicit. And probably the apparent fact that "we don't have children without mothers (parents)" is also meant to convey: we are good believers and take care of our children in accordance with the Quran. It is interesting to note how urgent it is to provide the children with substitute mothers and how little the biological mothers are able to look after their children in the best possible way for economic reasons. There are de facto many orphans in corresponding houses and many unhoused street children.

In some East African cities and countries, there are enormous gaps in the generations of extended families, mainly because of HIV. Often the parents of the children die of AIDS. Filiation is interrupted by all these deaths. In order to nevertheless pass on a part of what has happened, of the history of the deceased parents to the following generation, dying people sometimes write or draw reports about their lives for their children. This creates a certain minimal transmission.

This lack of parents, which causes untold suffering, also leads to a lack of conserving tradition. The gaps thus created can, in the best case, become a source of fruitful innovations.[12] This hypothesis, which starts from an extremely sad cause, can perhaps be understood as a kind of beacon of hope for the current cultural development of some East African countries. At best, new, less strictly determined cultural ways of life unfold in these terrible holes and gaps.

Parenthood in East African cities 31

Now follow four case vignettes which can illustrate what I have described and which also show how I can work with my basic psychoanalytical approach in East African cities, despite great cultural differences. I am talking here about people who "somehow survive" in psycho-somatic situations that make life hardly possible. And the smallest ones are of course the hardest hit and affected by what has been described so far. Freud (1926, p. 229): "Not true, the small living being is a rather miserable, powerless thing against the overpowering outside world, which is full of destructive influences."

Vignettes

The very traumatised little orphan girl in a tiny mirror

M, an approximately three-year-old severely traumatised little orphan girl who has come from the south of the country, does not want to draw. She looks at me for a while, unmoved, with a deadpan stare; she looks through me or avoids me entirely. I don't find her simply shy, as the carers tell me, but in a sense in deep revolt, in the midst of a silent inner cry. The beginning of an exchange between us only happens thanks to my little pocket mirror, which I give her and I am amazed at how interestedly, almost fascinatedly she looks at herself from all sides. This has nothing to do with vanity. She looks at herself, or actually studies herself, with great seriousness. Again and again she seems to discover something new about herself, about her reflection, to see, to study. And one thing leads to the study of another aspect of her face that has not yet been looked at and studied intensively enough or at all. She examines all possible facets, turning to let the light fall on them at different angles, wants to take them in and probably also memorise them. In Paulina Kernberg's (2008) book I came across the term "customs inspection", which very accurately describes what I observed in M.

After studying herself for some time and probably also searching for the face of her mother in the little mirror, which is so enlightening for her and obviously strengthens and stabilises her internally, composing and occupying her fragmented self, she closes the mirror gracefully and calmly and hands it back to me across the table. As she does so, she looks directly and freely into my face and eyes. Now I am perceived by her. Probably, thanks to the little mirror and thanks to my attentive presence, she has drawn closer to the representation of her inner mother. The enlivening of this inner image enables a positive projection onto me and thus an exchange with me. She probably looked for and found the face of her deceased mother in the mirror, on her own face. At any rate, this is indicated by the seriousness of her examination of her mirror image, insofar also of a part of herself or of her relationship to her mother. Peter Bründl (Munich) drew my attention to this important point. And of course something basic is added, namely my

32   *Parenthood in East African cities*

watching her while being present with all my senses open to her and occupying her, which thus becomes a containing, meaning-giving act.

Lacan (1949) assumes that our idea of our own body is that of a fragmented body, fragmented by our multiple inner fears of persecution. And in the mirror image, according to Lacan, the fragmented is put together, albeit in an illusory way, but still. This hypothesis describes quite well the action before and after the moments when M looks at herself in the mirror.

M's obvious obstinacy, which the home's management complains about, I understand as a bulwark, as it were, against painful, unbearable affects. It helps her to split off psychotic traumatisation fears, pain, losses and feelings of loneliness. The little orphan girl lost both her father and her mother to HIV/AIDS within a single year. She lived with them in the smallest possible space until one parent after the other died in agony. I only heard about this drama after the first hour of work with M, when I said to the head of the home that M must have experienced very bad things that she would not want to be reminded of under any circumstances. I took this also from my hardly bearable counter-transference during my first psychotherapeutic encounter with M. I experienced myself as blocked, desperate, powerless and helpless. I didn't know what to "do" next and saw myself as lonely and abandoned, i.e. all alone and forsaken. Only then did I have the idea to give M my little mirror. The head of the home also told me that the little girl spoke a dialect from the south that hardly anyone here understood. She is very intelligent and would be able to learn and speak the official language of the country in a flash. She simply refuses to do so. Her native language, her mother tongue, is indispensable for her, especially as a transitional object that functions as a bridge to a mother and a father both lost to her.

The little boy missing his father terribly

The second vignette. A colleague calls me to him on the stone benches, outside, in front of the main building of the psychiatric hospital. Opposite him sits an extraordinarily stately woman who seems to me like a mountain-shaped monument. She is covered from top to bottom with cloth and skirt. I sit down next to my colleague and see that on the left side a little "golden" smiling girl is, as it were, attached to the grandmother. She seems like an entirely accepted appendage of the grandmother. The two form a union; they are, as it were, fused. To the right of the grandmother, at some distance, which increases over the course of the therapeutic conversation, sits a little boy, K. He seems completely frightened. His face is taut, his mouth pressed together into a strip. K is frozen and does not dare to look at me. The colleague informs me briefly: "The boy is enuretic." The grandmother complains and complains and complains about the boy and of course I literally don't understand much of all this. But I can tell from her

Parenthood in East African cities   33

gestures and her agitation that she is very negative about the boy. The boy is bad, even with her, he doesn't study at school, wets the bed, he doesn't obey. Father and mother had separated and then left: the mother to another country, whereas the father went to the mainland. The father is not worth anything, says the grandmother (the mother's mother). He takes drugs and is a dealer. She can't depend on him at all. He doesn't give a damn about his child. Now and then, the boy and the girl, who is his sister, talk on the phone with one of their parents on Sundays.

I ask when the boy started wetting the bed at night. And it becomes clear that it started when he was separated from his parents, four years earlier. Since he has been living with his grandmother, he wets the bed at night.

K, the little boy, suffers from the loss of his parents, especially his father. He also suffers from his sister, who rivals him for the love of his grandmother. The sister clearly occupies a better position than K. She plays on this and mocks and ridicules her brother because of his so-called weaknesses. She says, for example, that he is stupid and very bad at school. I don't have the impression that the boy is stupid at all; on the contrary, he makes a bright and intelligent impression on me. He seems to be completely on his guard, he doesn't trust his surroundings. His longing for his father becomes clear, but at the same time his grandmother says that his father is not to be reckoned with at all, that he is a complete good-for-nothing.

I try to concentrate solely on K, which is not easy because the others, especially the little sister, often interfere. And K, for his part, is constantly moving away from contact with me. I look for him again and again and again, also with eye contact and especially with speaking contact. I always say his name before I approach something, introductory, calmly, benevolently, clearly and referring to him. In these moments he obviously realises immediately that I really mean him and perhaps experiences a somewhat different, more integrated sense of self. He is no longer just anyone, not just a negative appendage doing bad things. He sees himself perceived by me in a positive sense. The sister, as already mentioned, interferes and squeals, for example: he can't even write his own name. At the moment I am astonished and also a little frightened that he is unable to do that because it doesn't correspond to my image of him. K then writes his name and actually writes it a bit wrong. The middle letter is missing. At a later point, I study what he has written again at my leisure and wonder what he might have stumbled over. I see that he cannot write the M, the centre of his own name. The M is the first and most important letter in "Mama". Is he omitting and repressing mama? The boy is, of course, terribly ashamed of the mistake in his own name and the sister triumphs. What now?

I ask about his fears. First he says he has none. Then, after a long time: he is afraid of the night. I add that he is probably afraid of peeing in bed, but also of the bad and very painful blows from his grandmother.

34 *Parenthood in East African cities*

I ask if there is something he wants very much. He immediately says: "Yes, I want to come to Europe with you." He will repeat this at the beginning of each of our psychotherapeutic conversations. I reply that unfortunately I can't take him with me for various reasons. I want to leave him something of myself here. I think of a transitional object, but at the moment I don't know what to give, as I have practically nothing with me. I tear a sheet of paper out of my little book for notes, then fold it several times to make a kind of container inside. While I give him the folded paper, I say, "Look, maybe you can write something in there, what your secret is and what you wish for." K's expression brightens and he thanks me. He opens the page, takes my pencil and writes something inside. Then he closes everything and gives me the folded sheet. I ask him if I am really allowed to read it, since it is his secret. He tells me to read it. I open the various folds and inside the cavity of this multiply folded sheet is written: "BABO." Father.

The name is spelled correctly and with quite a confident ductus. Of course, I had also talked to him about his father. And he now locks his longing for his father in the secret compartment of his folded paper transitional object. I promise him that I will come back after a certain, not quite short time. And that we will then be able to see each other again.

I make a pact with the grandmother and tell her to swear to me that she will not hit the boy again. She swears with her hand. I now draw her "my picture" of the boy: K is not stupid but unhappy, he misses his father and mother. And I suggest to her to praise him when he doesn't wet the bed instead of beating him and demonising him, so to speak. In addition, I ask her for her address and telephone number so that she understands that I am in touch and mean what I say and also to see her handwriting.

When I am back in the country, at the second conversation, grandmother and aunt come along with the boy, and in addition, a female assistant stays near the bench where we are sitting. The women talk about K. K is surrounded by four women and refuses all cooperation. I tell him: "I don't think it's right for you to be alone among so many women. We want to stop here and make arrangements for next time. Methinks you wish very much that a man would be with you again." I myself thought of asking the colleague from the first conversation to assist the boy.

The next time, the third, K is accompanied by his father, whom his grandmother called a good-for-nothing, and who has come all the way here on a sea ferry. K beams and is overjoyed at his father's hand. The father looks prematurely aged, not particularly strong, rather a little bald and sickly. We talk together, the boy, his father and me. I finally explain to the father in detail how important he is for his boy and that I believe that his boy is also very important for him.

For the next meeting, the fourth, the day before I leave, the father does not want to agree to attend at first. The political situation is too difficult (there are political elections at the moment). Finally he says – maybe he will

Parenthood in East African cities   35

come after all. And he does come back the next time with his son, and it is obvious that the two of them have had some conflicts with each other in the meantime. K is a little less radiant. He again wants to come to Europe with me. And: his bed-wetting is over.

The therapeutic work described looked quite hopeless at the beginning. I would never have imagined, in accordance with the extremely negative image the grandmother gave me of the son-in-law, the father who was so important for the boy, that K's father would cooperate. He did.

Changing the "mother"

The third vignette. A grandmother comes to talk to her granddaughter, who is about 15 years old. The grandmother is an educated woman, a sought-after language teacher. The girl is very shy and full of shame, but at the same time bright and intelligent. Despite her age, she has been a bed-wetter for over a decade. In conversation, especially with the grandmother, because the girl speaks English very well although she cannot speak at first out of sheer shyness and shame, it soon became clear that it is mainly a separation problem. The bed-wetting apparently started the moment the girl was taken out of her family of origin and transferred to a single aunt. The aunt was apparently also supposed to be allowed to care for a child. However, the girl's mother gave birth to a boy at that time, to whom she probably wanted to devote herself intensively. The girl's wish now is to be allowed to go away from her aunt – she does not like her – to her grandmother. For the time being for the upcoming longer holidays, but actually for good. The grandmother agrees in principle to take the granddaughter to stay with her, although she works hard at her job. I explain to the grandmother and granddaughter how I understand the suffering of the young girl, namely as a consequence of being sent away, and emphasise the pain and also the anger of the girl, which consisted and still consists in seemingly being less worthy and less loved than, for example, her newborn brother. I talk about the possible symbolic meaning, the possible sense of bed-wetting, namely that the pee runs instead of crying, and suggest that perhaps the young woman feels the warmth of the urine and its own smell as home. Then I turn to the grandmother in particular and tell her that it would make sense if the girl's wish to live with her could be realised. And I ask whether she, who had agreed to take her granddaughter to live with her, could talk to her daughter and her family about it. If yes, she should emphasise that I consider this solution extremely important for the further development of the young woman and highly recommend it. The grandmother thinks that she can deal with this and take responsibility. We say goodbye with the possibility that the two of them can come again for a meeting during my next stay. Apparently, the young woman has not wet herself after two nights.

36   *Parenthood in East African cities*

This kind of psychotherapeutic conversation was of course only possible because the grandmother is an educated, largely independent, responsible woman who is interested in and concerned about her granddaughter's fate.

The confused, very young, pregnant woman

Now I am talking about a young woman in labour whose expressiveness shows how body language often tells us more, because it expresses more and more clearly than the spoken word. The spoken word is often used to cover up what spontaneous bodily expression can hardly conceal.

I work in the waking room with a confused, unresponsive, HIV-positive patient who is very pregnant with twins, about 18 years old, extremely beautiful and completely emaciated. She is confused and is treated with infusions to restore her fluid balance. She is completely dehydrated and has been in a patient's room for a long time, but apparently does not let anyone come near her and angrily turns everyone away.

The young, sick and pregnant woman was brought to this room from the rooms where up to 15 patients were staying with family members, some of them also lying on the floor and between the beds, because they did not know what to do. She is unresponsive, confused, her severely swollen tongue clogs her mouth and she writhes in convulsions. Fortunately, with each bag of "fluid" her condition improves. I try to reach her psychically and stand and move around her body, along the bed frame, gently and calmly saying her name at long intervals, holding her emaciated feet in my hands and giving them some ground with my hands. If there are any defensive movements on her part, I immediately stop myself. The patient becomes mentally clearer and clearer, begins to look into my eyes. I bend down to her eye level so as not to act from above. Suddenly she makes the tiniest of signs, either with one eye or one finger. Apparently my calling her name, my naming her, has reached her. Now a way has been found for an exchange that does not make her react resistively but makes her tune in. Now they want to insert a bladder probe into her and change the completely filthy bedclothes she is lying on. It is extremely rough going. I continue to call the patient's name and carefully hold her arms and also her head, not forcing at all, but still with some firmness. Suddenly she tries to rear up because the action on her and around her hurts her terribly. And she begins to growl rather loudly. I quickly realise that the situation is now very critical, because after the growling usually comes the biting. She is an HIV patient. And I immediately growl agitatedly, and at the same time intensely, the echo of her growl; I accompany her growl like a double. She calms down, no longer rears up, but hisses a word to the nursing staff.[13] I ask: "What is she saying?" They translate: "doucement", that is: please be more careful with me. In the evening, the young woman gave birth to twins, differently than planned, because they wanted to nurse her, so to speak, in order to do a caesarean section afterwards. The next day, in the morning, she leaves the hospital with her twins.

Notes

1 I am talking here about my psychoanalytical work in exclusively Muslim regions. When I mention the Quran, I always also mean the Hadiths, i.e. the books of interpretation that have been written for centuries for a better, more precise understanding of the Quran. The Quran, in its narrow interpretation, determines not only faith but also daily life and coexistence down to the last detail. Variants in the interpretation of the Quran or the faith are the basis for the different segments of believers within Islam: Sunnites, Shiites, Wahabis, Sufis, for example, as well as colourings of the faith based on natural religions. In East Africa, a Swahili-mixed Islam is often found, developed in the geographical and economic environment of coastal culture and the East–West trade in slaves and ivory. Mixed Islam means that the Quran in the narrower sense is supplemented and expanded by many other implications. These remarks on mixed Islam are based on oral reports by Al Imfeld (Zurich), an outstanding Africa expert, journalist and writer.
2 Of course, the European one is not a uniform model either!
3 At least nowadays – by the majority.
4 This is especially true for the social lower and middle classes.
5 Islam implies law in many interpretations of the Quran.
6 There are culturally standardised preparations before and for marriage. Man and woman learn different things separately. The woman learns – from an experienced, unrelated woman – to serve her husband, to provide for him and to make his life easier. The future husband is prepared by his father to be a husband.
7 Here, too, changes are underway. I see this in the medical records, which increasingly include precise dating.
8 For "the whites" there are specific, pejorative names in every national language, which usually have something to do with the respective former colonies. For example, where the French colonised the country, the white foreigners are now called "frenchis".
9 In Western European societies, a well-known legal statement has long been: *mater semper certa, pater incertus*. In Islamic cultures it sounds different. The father, the most important and powerful man in the family structure, is attributed the status of *certus*.
10 Of course, there are variations here too. Girls are not genitally mutilated in all countries.
11 Children often come to psychiatric hospitals whose main trigger for illness is probably this "transplanting". They feel like relegated children who are apparently worth less to their parents than their siblings.
12 Creativity does not arise from abundance, but if at all, from lack, as Freud, but also Bion and others describe.
13 The staff are not trained.

Bibliography

Charlier, M. (2006). Geschlechtsspezifische Entwicklung in patriarchalisch-islamischen Gesellschaften und deren Auswirkungen auf den Migrationsprozess. *Psyche – Zeitschrift für Psychoanalyse* 60(2): 97–117.

38 Parenthood in East African cities

Freud, S. (1919). *Wege der psychoanalytischen Therapie*. Studienausgabe. Ergänzungsband. Frankfurt am Main: Fischer.

Freud, S. (1926). *Hemmung, Symptom und Angst*. Studienausgabe, vol. VI. Frankfurt am Main: Fischer.

Hirsi Ali, A. (2015). *Reformiert Euch! Warum der Islam sich ändern muss*. München: Knaus.

Kernberg, P. (2008). *Spiegelbilder*. Stuttgart: Klett-Cotta.

Lacan, J. (1949). Das Spiegelstadium als Bildner der Ichfunktion wie sie uns in der psychoanalytischen Erfahrung erscheint. In: J. Lacan (Ed.), *Schriften*, vol. 1 (selected and ed. V. Haas, new 3rd corrected ed.). Weinheim/Berlin: Quadriga: 61–70 [Report for the 16th International Congress for Psychoanalysis in Zürich on 17 July 1949].

Parin, Paul (1985). *Zu viele Teufel im Land. Aufzeichnungen eines Afrikareisenden*. Frankfurt am Main: Syndikat.

Parin, P., Morgenthaler, F. and Parin-Matthèy, G. (1972). *Die Weissen denken zu viel. Psychoanalytische Untersuchungen in Westafrika*. München: Kindler.

Pradelles de Latour, C.-H. (1997). *Le crâne qui parle*. Deuxième édition de Ethnopsychanalyse en pays bamiléké. Paris: EPEL.

Pradelles de Latour, C.-H. (2014). *La dette symbolique. Thérapies traditionnelles et psychanalyse*. Paris: EPEL.

Racamier, P.-C. (1993). *Le psychanalyste sans divan. La psychanalyse et les institutions de soins psychiatriques*. Bibliothèque Scientifique Payot. Paris: Payot.

Saegesser, Barbara (2014). Psychoanalytische Arbeit mit BB's, Kleinkindern und Müttern in unterschiedlichen afrikanischen Ländern (Le travail psychanalytique avec les bébés, des petits enfants et des mères dans divers pays d'Afrique). *Schweizerische Gesellschaft für Psychoanalyse (SGPsa) Bulletin* No. 77 (Spring): 5–13.

Wohlfahrt, E. and Özbek, T. (2006). Eine ethnopsychoanalytische Kasuistik über das Phänomen der Besessenheit. *Psyche – Zeitschrift für Psychoanalyse* 60(2): 118–130.

5 School systems and school visits in East African cities and rural areas

Madrasas

The first training, formerly reserved for little boys alone, and now for all little Muslim girls too, from about four years old, is to work in a madrasa, i.e. a Quranic school. This participation costs nothing and is almost vital, since state and religion are interrelated. If children do not go there, their family can be seen as hostile and as a non-Quranic one and socially isolated.

Originally, certainly from the Middle Ages onwards, and probably also before, madrasas were considered places of instruction for Islam and later as training centres for certain fields of knowledge that are presented in the Quran, such as those of Islamic law: Fiqh. At that time, these places, for which very ornate buildings were often donated and erected – some of these buildings are still standing today – were considered very exclusive training centres for young men, who of course grew older during their school years and could also learn and take up professions, e.g. that of the Imam. Other training institutions on an Islamic basis were rare. Christian missionaries came across this striking gap in education. They offered training and also so-called higher education, similar to the European courses of study. Whereas, the Islam-linked training often emphasised that everything important was in the Quran and that other training could not bring anything new or interesting. This argument, that everything important is in the Quran, is held responsible for the comparatively low education of people, for example in East African countries. The educational background of Muslims seems to be much higher when they live in regions of other faiths than when they live in their "own" regions.

Now back to the madrasa for the little ones. Here, the young children learn parts of the Quran by heart, mostly mainly suras. This is probably their first access to the Arabic, albeit the High Arabic, language (understood and/or spoken only by extraordinarily educated or religiously attached people) and to the Quran. Afterwards, they are not able to speak or read Arabic or understand the contents of the Quran they have learnt, but can at best reproduce what they have learnt by heart, by ear.

DOI: 10.4324/9781003451587-5

40 *School systems and visits in East African cities and rural areas*

Attendance at the madrasa lasts approximately from two to four years. It is probably compulsory insofar as there is certainly social control over attendance. Nowadays, thanks to this participation, individual Arabic words can at least be understood and used to some extent, but it is the case, even for people with an academic education, that if they want to read the Quran in the original texts – with many commentaries – they must first learn the language High Arabic *à fond*. Memorising Quranic verses by ear, as it were, gives a taste of High Arabic, nothing more.

In West Africa, the colonies did not tolerate madrasas. Madrasas were only introduced there after the withdrawal of the colonists.

In some countries today, there are madrasas for boys and for girls. In one photo I have seen, the boys sit in front and the girls at a great distance behind them. I don't know if boys and girls can go to the madrasa together in other East African countries. I assume that this is not possible in all East African countries. Tanzania is considered relatively open-minded in some respects, perhaps because a large Christian community lives there and many tourists come there.

Schools in farmland

Many children in East Africa go to school mainly because they get something to eat there. When schools close or teachers are not present, which is more often the case, some children do not have enough to eat.

Many children cannot go to school because they lack even the minimum amount of money to be dressed in such a way that their parents are not ashamed. Not infrequently, parents do not have enough money to buy the child a pencil and some paper. There are many understandable reasons on the part of parents and children (children have to help their parents with the rural work) to prevent the children from attending school. In comparison with other children, not only the parents are ashamed but also the children, who see themselves as inferior and poor.

And many teachers see themselves as too badly paid (which is true) and find their work, especially in rural East Africa, extremely difficult and exhausting. I hear this especially from the south of Ethiopia. It often happens that teachers are absent from classes, even for long periods of time, which is not something out of the ordinary but seems to be part of the job description.

The Coronavirus pandemic, which has been going on for more than a year, has deepened the poor education situation also in East Africa. Some children give up learning at school and look for paid work. Continuous reliable basic schooling is unfortunately not available. This may not only be true for rural areas but also for urban housing estates and neighbourhoods where mainly poorer to very poor people live in tin-roof huts (if in any kind of structure at all). I am thinking here of the huge cities with millions of inhabitants such as Cairo (approx. 10 million inhabitants and 5 million in slums around it), Alexandria (approx. 6 million inhabitants), Addis Ababa (approx. 4 million inhabitants) and Dar es Salaam (approx. 5 million inhabitants).

Foreign languages are taught in schools. They are often the languages of the former colonies. For example, English in Ethiopia, Sudan and Tanzania; French in Djibouti; Italian in Somalia, etc. People often have difficulties with these European languages, even though they learn/hear them at school, just as they do in Europe. Whereby it can be assumed that teaching in East African countries is comparatively much less regulated.

In principle, I know certain facts about schools mainly from hearsay and from brief conversations with students. I have never looked at textbooks, but rely on statements made by Konstantin Schreiber (2019) in his descriptions of Egyptian textbooks, where he also brings in experts to assess the books under discussion and all of them emphasise how far from neutral the history books are. For example, regarding all the wars with Israel and how indirectly criticisms of Christian thoughts and rules as well as of Jewish thoughts and rules always flow into the descriptions of historical events. A kind of division between "us" (Muslims) and the "others" (Jews and Christians) is evident.

Psychological lines of development usually go hand in hand with schooling in Europe and other Western countries. For me, in the East African environment, such developmental lines can only be described approximately. I cannot describe the phases as precisely as "Western" child development psychology likes to. If I think in terms of Freudian phases, I recognise above all the oral phase in boys and also intensive narcissistic fixations. And I see a clear difference between females, who tend more towards compulsion, and males, who tend more towards oral narcissism and grandiose ego/self-development possibilities.

A son is much more welcome in this world structured by Muslim religion and politics, already at birth, than a girl. A celebration is staged for the birth of the son, but not for the girl. He undergoes circumcision soon after, and there is also an occasion for festivities. The boy is strongly attached to both parents, especially to the father, who is very proud of his son. At the same time, he is strongly attached to his mother, because the birth of a son increases her social weight. The boy, like the man, husband, father, is granted much more freedom than the girl is. Not every boy has to help in the household; maybe occasionally he must help the father, if he has a manual profession or is a farmer etc. In addition, I often encountered boys who do not learn a trade but, especially where it is convenient, for example when drugs transport routes run nearby, buy drugs, which is often paid for by their mothers. I imagine that the same would not be possible for a girl and that the mother would not pay for drugs for her girl.

Girls are closely bound to their mothers by socio-religious rules and regulations. The mother watches and controls her girls, also in the sense that she has to pay attention to their purity. The girl is not allowed to have close contact with a boy. At the age of four to five, the girl is genitally mutilated.

As soon as she has survived this terrible ordeal and has come through it to some extent, the girl is considered a woman. More precisely, she is a woman from the moment when her sexual pleasure capacity and the prerequisite for a largely easy birth have been almost destroyed. And the next step to becoming/being a woman is to marry a man.

The parallel does not apply to the boy: a boy is not a man only when he marries, although this may play a role in his standing as a manly man. Of course, in the Quran, both the mother and the father are expected, socially and religiously, to love their children. The social-religious side of culture is very much in the foreground, especially in the case of the girl. I think that girls stick to their mothers mainly for social reasons. Depending on the case, this may also be to protect them from the father, but not necessarily out of love.

Girls and women are punished more severely if they take a step outside the social structures. They are shunned, ostracised and, in cases of adultery, stoned to death, depending on the circumstances. Women who expect and give birth to a child out of wedlock are also ostracised. In larger cities, new-born babies are found at night or in the morning, which unmarried mothers have to throw away, so to speak, in order to survive themselves. I have also worked with discarded children.

East African families live in the framework of extended families that can be geographically very far apart. In East Africa it is sometimes the custom, when one's own family becomes too large, for example when a man marries a new wife or new children are born, to pass on one or two members of the family to another part of the family where there is no surplus of people. For example, to a single aunt. This is a procedure that is hardly imaginable today in Western regions. I worked with female patients and also a male patient who had been moved in this way because of problems in the family of origin, for example a new third wife of the father. In another case I remember, it was only when the girl was sent away from home at the age of 17 that bed-wetting occurred within a few days. She was a very discriminating young woman, who wanted to study later. After three meetings, she did not wet her bed any more. She felt quite content afterwards, because the aunt with whom she was now to live obviously seemed to be a loving enough, interesting and also intellectually interested woman.

Now I present the psychoanalytic work I did in walking and sitting with AB, who was sent far away by his family.

Of course, he also had problems at school, because he was always transferred to a completely different environment and encountered different schools, teachers and schoolmates.

The psychoanalytic psychotherapies and processes that I describe can be better understood if I also depict the respective different environment at

School systems and visits in East African cities and rural areas   43

the same time. Here, in East Africa, I am dealing with a completely different psychiatric milieu, precisely because of religious Islamic, Sunni and somewhat "peculiar"-seeming basic ethnic rules and influences. For this reason, too, deviations from the classical psychoanalytical approach are unavoidable. This psychoanalytical approach requires creativity not only within the respective framework and process, but also, or so I have experienced, in relation to the external framework.

How to work at all? Where to work? Somewhere to work quietly and alone is not often readily available in some ethnic groups and societies that live close together. I want to work with my patients away from the other patients and the nursing staff, and I am always looking for a new place where a certain confidentiality can develop. Sometimes such a place cannot be found, but is situated in the midst of other people. And these others tend to interfere after a while and want to join in.

Vignette: the boy without a home

Mr. B greets me very warmly on my second visit to the Mental Hospital and tells me he has two patients for me, two young men. He shows me the two of them outside in the lounge, a crumbling loggia made of stone. Here I can see the currently present – there are of course also chronic – male patients and, if I choose to, wish them good day. All the others seem to be much older and, due to severe drug abuse, in some cases much more physically degraded than the young patients assigned to me. And Mr. B insists on telling me important things the next morning, when he starts work. The next day, in the morning, I wait outside on a stone bench for Mr. B., who wanted to tell me something urgent. A psychological trainee from the mainland and AB, one of the two young patients, are also waiting for him. I had only had very brief contact with AB the day before, without having already made an appointment for the next day. How AB comes here at this time of the morning, exactly where I am, surprises me and is quite inexplicable to me at first. In retrospect, I can understand it as an expression of his form of transference love, which, it seems, flared up very quickly the evening before, and which apparently makes him particularly cunning and inventive (like Ulysses)! He sits down next to me, silent and seemingly unconcerned, plagued by severe side effects from the haloperidol. He trembles, falls asleep abruptly, slurs his words, can't quite keep his saliva in his mouth, keeps losing his posture, can hardly walk. I describe his current condition in such detail so that it becomes clear which overdoses the patients have to suffer depending on the situation.

The psychology trainee observes him, gives me a look and says somewhat deprecatingly, "He's autistic." I reply that even if he were autistic, it would be possible to find an approach to him. Ever since I sat here on the stone bench that morning, I have heard a kitten meowing piteously and

44 *School systems and visits in East African cities and rural areas*

screaming incessantly. No one reacts. I ask the three people around me – in the meantime another young psychological trainee, who also comes from the mainland, has joined us – if they also hear the meowing. Yes. Me: "It's obviously coming from the nearest room. Is there any way to open this room?" After some hesitation, the budding psychologist wants to get the key to the padlock. She opens the door. A small, skinny, completely dishevelled kitten jumps out, meowing and panicking. Once again, no one seems to take any notice of this pitifully small and whining kitten that seems to be starving and dying of thirst. For me, this indifference towards the suffering creature is also emblematic of the lack of attention and the non-existent narcissistic occupation of the patients, who are more like inmates who are kept quiet and hardly "treated", or just not treated at all.

Unexpectedly, the young patient AB grabs the kitten by the neck fur and sits it on his shoulder. I get scared, because it seems to me that the chances are 50/50 whether he is really worried about the little kitten or whether he will kill it. At the same time, it shows how familiar he is with small animals and how he probably tries to empathise with their conditions. He, the apparent "psychotic", unlike the budding psychologists, does not behave indifferently. He probably does all this because of his very quickly unfolding positive transference to me. I ask for some water and something to eat for the kitten, e.g. from the kitchen in the men's section. There is nothing edible there at this time, according to the psychologists. The young trainee now digs out two biscuits from her bag and the kitten eats a little. I then ask her again to take the kitten to the kitchen and see if there is some water or milk around. AB sits the tiny, skinny, nervous, mercurial bundle on his shoulders again, walks towards the kitchen and comes back later, without a kitten and without making a sound. I am worried but say nothing at that moment, wondering if the kitten is still alive. I try to explain to the psychological trainees how important animals can be for patients and that the way a patient perceives animals and takes care of them can say something about his psychological state. For example, about their ability to develop a certain empathy towards living beings. The budding psychologists to whom I am supposed to teach something listen relatively unmoved. This almost provocative lack of interest in new points of view also has to do with the fact that I am a woman and a non-coloured person (I have the skin colour of the former colonists), and one tends not to want to absorb much (nothing!) from them because of the hatred they attract.

AB, as already described, probably because of the haloperidol, can hardly move, can hardly articulate anything and falls asleep from one minute to the next. When he is not asleep, he listens carefully to what I talk about with others and, interestingly, he understands the meaning of what I talk about easily and quickly. For example, if I describe something with humour, he is sometimes the only one who understands and starts laughing in a flash.

School systems and visits in East African cities and rural areas   45

From this point of view, he participates in what is happening and is able to follow the intellectual detail in a conversation.

On one of the next days, he pulls a licking stick out of the pocket of his trainer trousers. He enjoys licking and sucking it and suddenly offers for me to suck it too. He repeats this two or three times and each time I say, no, thank you. He is literally attached to me and I suspect a strong positive transference and possibly a regressive movement towards a dependency problem. If I assume a form of transference that idealises me, there is of course a chance that this can suddenly tip over into the opposite. Fortunately, this did not happen during my short stay. Once I noticed how he looked very closely into my backpack when I opened it and it was lying open next to me. I think he would have liked to reach in and take something of mine out for himself. But he didn't.

I have not been able to see AB's medical records. In order to obtain the relevant handwritten notes, each of which would be barely legible to me, I would waste a lot of time just looking for and finding the person who arranges the handwritten notes under discussion. Paper files are collected in many high, yellowing piles.

I receive verbal information about AB's background from two sources. On the one hand from Mr. B, who explains to me: AB came to the clinic because he is said to have hit his mother (actually his aunt). And apparently he was aggressive towards other people; for example, in the huge market he apparently hit them as well, depending on the situation. Two years ago, AB was given away by his mother from the mainland and went to the island – to his aunt – and at the same time the aunt gave her daughter to her sister on the mainland.

I am present during a conversation between Mr. B and the aunt with whom AB was staying. She complains and complains and complains about her bad young nephew. Methinks she is desperate to get rid of him. And she refers to his grandmother, who already had a mental illness. Her manic accusatory speech probably covers up – defensively – a paranoid disorder, and in addition she is extremely self-centred, very narcissistic. Probably the diagnosis – in a European understanding – of a personality disorder would be appropriate. The problems of her young nephew are apparently none of her business.

At the same time, quasi-incidentally, I get a hint from a former neighbour of AB's, who also lived on the mainland, about his mother's relationship with him. AB's mother apparently couldn't stand him very well. She had constantly put him down. Nothing was right about what he did. She had never been satisfied with the patient and had constantly scolded and abused him. He was probably a disturbing factor for her, a negative self-object. How it came about, I can't say.

Back to AB. During this common waiting time of about an hour for Mr. B, AB stays around me all the time, as far as this is possible. He waits for me in the morning when I come, and in different places, without

46 School systems and visits in East African cities and rural areas

disrupting my work. He seems to have chosen some spots from which to spy me. He has, as already mentioned, obviously very quickly developed a positive, probably idealising transference towards me. There are moments when he looks at me, studies me and gazes immovably into my eyes with his wide-open big eyes and wants to deepen his gaze as if into my eyes, actually immerse himself. And depending on that, a little panic suddenly rises up in me and I think: "Watch out, now it could be dangerous." The moment I realise that, I guess I automatically move away from him a little bit. As already mentioned, he has not attacked me directly or indirectly during the whole time he has been near me.

AB's medication dose is becoming more and more bearable for him – though maybe he has also dropped the medication – and more adapted to his situation. My psychotherapeutic work with this psychiatric patient takes place outside: either while walking, when he accompanies me from one building within the psychiatric complex to another, or sitting in the open air on stone slabs and benches. The rooms available are in fact gloomy, not inviting, half-decaying, not protective, but rather somewhat threatening in their gloomy appearance combined with the scantiest cleanliness or hygiene. Mostly the complex consists of corridors, where quite a few other people pass by or sit along the walls. If I go somewhere where AB can't come, I tell him and he accepts without reacting aggressively.

On the third day or so, he comes with a present for me, a sheet of paper showing, on both sides and in colour, all the fish and fish-like animals that swim or live in the Indian Ocean. I thank him. On the second-to-last day of our collaboration, I return the "fish leaf" to him. He comes to meet me in the morning with two younger children and says they are his siblings. No one had informed me of this. Neither did he. I give him back his gift and he immediately passes it on to his siblings. Here again, one of his gestures shows how much he is in principle in exchange and how strong his desire to make amends is. As with Y (see the vignette in Chapter 1), it looks as if he can move from the schizoid-paranoid to the depressive position in a short time, or at least in between them.

The aunt, whom I saw and heard talking to Mr. B, strikes me as someone who is a poor listener and constantly talks about herself and her own problems. The biological mother often seems to hate the patient. He can't please her. She seems to treat him very badly. So part of my psychoanalytical therapeutic work with AB, apart from positive mirroring and containing and not questioning him – especially narcissistically – can also be understood in such a way that he reacts negatively to his mother and aunt and probably sees himself as rejected. The previous mothers would be – are for him – the not good family members and I would be the new sufficiently good mother. This possibility of his to divide into good and bad, actually his form of defence, naturally makes my short work with him easier. My presence is a kind of elixir of life for him, thanks to this idealised

School systems and visits in East African cities and rural areas   47

transference form, and enables him to unfold the narcissism of life. AB is getting better every day. And he can bear to share me with others. He sits next to me, and if someone comes to discuss something with me, he goes away for a while of his own accord. Sometimes several young patients sit around me and he is, in a circle, one among others. Gradually, he joins other young patients, sits outside with them at the stone table, talks, eats and laughs with them.

AB wants to write something in my notebook, in which I often write down something, which he has obviously observed. The felt-tip pen I can give him is drying up. So today, when I write it down, I can't easily read and reproduce the whole text. He writes in English, so not in his mother tongue but in a foreign language:

> My name is AB.
> I come from Bongo; D. e. S.
> I come from Bongo,
> I like soda and chicken and cook.
> I like a basketball and football
> I like a mother I like a father

That sounds quite basic, but because of the foreign language, it denotes no small effort. He probably wants to show me what he can do, what he has learned and who he is. And he silently wishes, albeit scenically, that I would take him with me to my country in my notebook, inside my backpack.

Towards the end of this somewhat unusual therapy, we are sitting outside in the garden on an old wooden bench, and AB takes small objects out of the pocket of his trainer trousers: a sweet, a stone, a tiny scrap of paper, a sweet wrapper and other very small things, and shows them to me. Suddenly he carefully pulls out a razor blade. Now I'm beginning to think it's a bit dangerous. He takes the razor blade to cut off small protruding short threads on his trainer trousers. He cleans himself up, so to speak, or makes himself beautiful, although of course I don't know what these little threads and tangles, which are torn-up trainer material, mean to him. Does he perceive them as aggressive and threatening or does he want to look better or more well-groomed, i.e. less dilapidated? When he stops, he suddenly begins to cut his fingernails with this razor blade, which is not framed but raw and flexible and probably extremely sharp. This is too much for me. I can see that he is doing it skilfully, and certainly not for the first time. I can't stand this action, which seems so dangerous and at the same time self-endangering to me, I can hardly look at it, I'm afraid he might cut himself or turn against me. AB is completely absorbed in his fingernail care. I stand up and walk a few steps away. The image cuts into me. I am startled. Shortly afterwards, fortunately, one of the rare

48   *School systems and visits in East African cities and rural areas*

groomers comes by, and I ask him to take the razor blade away from AB. He does so and I say goodbye to AB.

The other patient Mr. B had told me about shows little interest in joining me and his inmates in unorganised, free-flowing conversations. He is very marked by his addiction.

Bibliography

Charlier, M. (2006). Geschlechtsspezifische Entwicklung in patriarchalisch-islamischen Gesellschaften und deren Auswirkung auf den Migrationsprozess. *Psyche – Zeitschrift für Psychoanalyse* 60(2): 97–117.

Freud, S. (1926). *Hemmung, Symptom und Angst*. Studienausgabe, vol. VI. Frankfurt am Main: Fischer.

Hirsi Ali, A. (2015). *Reformiert euch! Warum der Islam sich ändern muss*. München: Knaus.

Kernberg, P. (2008). *Spiegelbilder*. Stuttgart: Klett-Cotta.

Lacan, J. (1949). Das Spiegelstadium als Bildner der Ichfunktion wie sie uns in der psychoanalytischen Erfahrung erscheint. In: J. Lacan (Ed.), *Schriften*, vol. 1 (selected and ed. V. Haas, new 3rd corrected ed.). Weinheim/Berlin: Quadriga: 61–70 [Report for the 16th International Congress for Psychoanalysis in Zürich on 17 July 1949].

Racamier, P.-C. (1993). *Le Psychanalyste sans divan. La psychanalyse et les institutions de soins psychiatriques*. Bibliothèque Scientifique Payot. Paris: Payot.

Saegesser, Barbara (2014). Psychoanalytische Arbeit mit BB's, Kleinkindern und Müttern in unterschiedlichen afrikanischen Ländern (Le travail psychanalytique avec les bébés, des petits enfants et des mères dans divers pays d'Afrique). *Schweizerische Gesellschaft für Psychoanalyse (SGPsa) Bulletin* No. 77 (Spring): 5–13.

Saegesser, Barbara (2015). Psychoanalytische Feldarbeit in ostafrikanischen Städten. In: Peter Bründl and Carl E. Scheidt (Eds.), *Spätadoleszenz. Identitätsprozesse und kultureller Wandel*. Frankfurt am Main: Brandes & Apsel: 211–238.

Saegesser, Barbara (2016). Koranische Normen und Psychotherapie. *Tribune Psychanalytique* 14.

Schreiber, Konstantin (2019). *Kinder des Koran. Was muslimische Schüler lernen*. Berlin: Ullstein.

Spitz, René A. and Wolf, Katherine M. (1946). Anaclitic depression: an inquiry into the genesis of psychiatric conditions in early childhood, II. *The Psychoanalytic Study of the Child* 2(1): 313–342.

6 The baby and the child without a mother

Isn't it true, the little living being is a rather poor, powerless thing against the overpowering outside world, which is full of destructive influences.

(Freud, 1926, p. 229)

My external psychoanalytical frame, my internal psychoanalytical frame

I often worked as a humanitarian psychoanalyst in different East African countries during shorter stays (during my holidays from my own practice). In this way I got to know culturally different living and working situations. The attitude towards professionally trained humanitarian helpers is often very ambivalent here, for various reasons. There is a generalised distrust of so-called knowledgeable whites. The author and comprehensive Africa expert Jean Ziegler (2016) even speaks of hatred of and towards whites, which is not entirely unjustified if we also understand the configuration as an unconscious one. As a humanitarian European psychoanalyst, I often trigger the following ambivalences or resistances in the environment.

On the one hand, there is a general fear of the white people, who know everything better, who tell you what to do, who order you around, who bring your programmes, and who make you feel ashamed and small. The white people who don't let you do things the way you want to. And at the same time, in many East African countries, especially in the more south-eastern ones, I know there is, and I experience, an identification with the former aggressors, the colonists. Frantz Fanon (1963/1961) researched and wrote about this identification with the colonists.

As soon as I turn my attention to individual children or a group, the child's attention is usually quickly diverted away from me and drawn to other persons. Children, orphanage children and children in hospital are supposed to narcissistically support the adults who are also deprived, and if they get involved with someone else, for example with me, jealousy immediately arises in the environment, among the aid workers who are also shortchanged and usually live in the poorest social circumstances. The rather unhappy and depressed helpers and midwives in the various

DOI: 10.4324/9781003451587-6

50   *The baby and the child without a mother*

organisations and partly also in the hospitals understandably want some attention too. They demand narcissistic attention from the little ones and say: kiss me, hug me, say mummy. In this respect, it is also very important for my work to find a suitable approach to the care team.

Of course, my external frame for my psychoanalytical work cannot correspond to a European external frame. In East African countries I practically never have a quiet room where I can withdraw with the little patients. With the babies I stay anyway in the familiar place where their small bed is, except for those who are always locked in the dark. (The latter practice probably has cultural reasons for it.) I try to take the little ones outside into the air so they can see and smell the bright sky and some plants and hear the birds whistling. This is seen all around as a rather strange thing to do. However, the polysensitivity of the youngest children can develop better this way and at best lead to curiosity about the world. Or I choose a small, quiet corner within the orphanage organisation and work in a distant presence to the others. Above all, the other children become curious this way and soon turn to me themselves. There are situations without a quiet corner: for instance in the tents of Médecins Sans Frontières. I have offered my help if they can use me. I am called in when they can no longer cope with the psychological problems of the mothers and babies. And there I sit down on the footstool of the woman who has fled and who currently has more difficult problems than the others, and all the others – including the carers – look and listen. Depending on the relationship situation to be dealt with, this can be extremely unusual and extremely uncomfortable for me.

In my opinion, the external framework also includes a list of the most common psychosomatic illnesses to be expected in orphanage and hospital children and infants: all children are deprived and traumatised and show hospitalism symptoms or syndromes: i.e. reactions after severe traumatisation, malnutrition (physical and psychological), increased susceptibility to illness and mortality, increased incidence of infectious diseases. In all the East African countries I visited, from the north to the southeast, to the border between Somalia and Ethiopia, the orphans and those in neonatology usually had severe bronchitis to pneumonia and more or less chronic diarrhoea. Eating disorders, motor slowdown, great irritability and at the same time apathy were common (see Spitz and Wolf 1946), as were contact and perception disorders with autistic features. There were also stereotypies such as wagging the head, swaying, swaying oneself on the knees; self-injuries, such as banging the head against the wall or hard objects; intellectual and emotional retardation; as well as mental retardation, which can be like pseudo-debility. And unfortunately, as a consequence, a limited ability to learn and thus problems at school, if they reach it at all, which later leads to a socially weak position, and makes climbing the social ladder almost impossible.

My inner psychoanalytical frame

I have to "situationally adapt" my place of work; here I work psychoanalytically without a couch and without a fixed external setting: no room, no couch, no chair, no quietness, no exchange in a two-person situation is fixed. My psychoanalytic frame is my inner psychoanalytic frame. Psychanalysis arises in the inner psychoanalytic process, which can be more or less independent of space and time – not only as philosophically but also as concretely understood. I open all my senses to see and to go on a journey to understand little by little the patient, to come – inside – nearer to him and at the time always maintain my inner distance. I can be a double to him, I can be a mirror for him, I can feel and understand many pieces of what he is thinking and feeling himself, but I still stay myself and hold an inner distance, which is indispensable for the psychoanalytical work I do. If I am not able to hold this very inner distance, I lose the way to allow the psychoanalytical work to become fruitful. Or in other words: I try to give the patient the chance to find, himself, by his creativity, his fruitful, perhaps new, way.

I again try to give the little one its space, although or because, due to the all-round traumatic and traumatising situation, it is about to withdraw completely and no longer experience any desires. André Green (2007, 2011) calls these anti-movements "passivation". If the baby or the infant is left alone, it steadily moves towards its own death. In this situation I become, at best, a kind of double for the short time I am available for working with the babies (Golse and Roussillon 2015). I try to encounter the anaclitic depression of the little ones by narcissistically occupying and approaching these children, seeking them with my gaze, looking at them, talking to them. The seeking is meant literally, because they cower, either in the cot, behind the other children or even behind a smiling mask (see the vignette about Z below). My clinical experience in East African orphanages and state hospitals, in a extremely deprived milieu, shows me that the development of a defence against a part of the too-intrusive environmental impressions, i.e. the life-threatening object influences, becomes effective very early in the newborn and in the baby, much earlier than psychoanalysts thought for a long time. It is possible that psychic defences, mainly dissociations – apart from the psychotic episodes – can already begin prenatally, for example in the form of retarded development or a developmental standstill.

Nowadays it seems to be verified by experiments not only that babies have the five senses operating before and after birth, but from the moment their eyes can open, they see and react to, in the uterus, special signs that emerge in the uterus. Since the uterus is not closed, there is some light entering in, shining through his limits and the baby can perceive different things. All these functions are the baby's main "instruments" to be able to adapt "somehow" to the new environment, which is very different from the

52 *The baby and the child without a mother*

intrauterine one, to survive and to orientate itself in a minimal way. A perinatal baby seeks protection from internal and external threats. I am thinking of psychotic fears and also protection from excessively intrusive, i.e. destructive, environmental signals. It seems to me, according to my observations, that such protective mechanisms are particularly pronounced or expressive and thus impressive in babies who are deprived extremely early.

In addition to the vignettes presented below, see also "The very traumatised little orphan girl in a tiny mirror" in Chapter 4.

Vignettes

Z hidden behind her mask

Here is my first clinical example of dissociation, defence against the environment for psychological survival, in a girl who is probably barely one year old. Her name is Z. In the large visitors' room of an East African orphanage, babies and small children lie on the floor. The older ones play on the floor while visitors, in their street shoes, more or less skilfully walk around the children on this very floor. I look at the little ones, see their reactions to me, the "white one" coming towards them in a friendly way. I notice a pretty little girl lying smiling in the middle of this more or less full floor area, smiling continuously and appearing completely relaxed. I wonder how the little girl is doing this, living so well in this dangerous, chaotic, interconnected mess of partly extremely large (to her) feet and crawling roommates.

With a culturally very frequently used word, I seek contact, saying "you pretty one" to her in Arabic. No, she does not react; even when I repeat my chant, nothing happens. Now I touch her feet very lightly. No reaction. However, contrary to the relaxed impression I have of her, I realise that her feet are very tense and hard. Only now can I understand more, so to speak, and I see that she is dissociating. Clinically, I now proceed in the way I have developed and introduced in the various African countries. I choose the place for skin contact furthest away from the head, the feet. I give them support, form a feather-light base with my hands, a kind of container for their feet. Z moves a little. Finally, after about two days, she wakes up from her dreamy state, recognises me immediately when I enter the big room, crawls to me, which she couldn't physically do before, and she wants to be with me. And from now on she also hits me or tries to bite me as well as all the other little orphanage residents and competitors who want to come near me. One could say that the instinct to take over (Freud 1905) has reorganised itself in a flash, the aggressive impulses form and the little one begins, thanks to this happening, to get herself out of her passivity and to actively fight for her place in life and for her life.

After working with Z five times, she immediately sees me when I enter the large room, moves and tries to crawl near me and finally makes successful attempts to walk. All this relates to her new desire to get close to me and to share with me. In the beginning of our psychoanalytical work, she didn't feel any desires. And now, with her emerging wishes, she becomes angrier at the others who also come or are near me. The stereotype of smiling recedes.

I go from the assumption that psychism is already present from birth. Based on my clinical experience, like Bernard Golse, I am by no means of the opinion that a newborn or even a developing child *in utero* is only a white sheet of paper to be described by the primary caregiver, e.g. also by means of their fantasies. I observe psychic self-movements, as well as the one just described. In the same rhythm as with the development of psychosomatic abilities and skills, the learning of how to configure and strengthen the narcissism of life, conversely the degradation of important cognitive, psychic, psychosomatic structures increases if there is no sufficiently nourishing (understood in the broadest sense of the word) environment. In the negative case, the little one literally crawls into itself and in the furthest corner of the small bed falls silent. The narcissism of death or the work of the drive of death (Freud 1920) reigns much earlier than is usually described. Whereas Spitz and Wolf (1946), with their concept of anaclitic depression, implicitly speak of such fatal withdrawal movements. If the object is not sufficiently good, this retreat into illness and into psychological and also somatic dying begins. Of the orphanage and hospital babies in these East African countries where I worked, 95% are not only physically extremely undernourished, for example completely dehydrated and malnourished, and consequently already ill at the time of their birth, so that the gastrointestinal tract and the respiratory tract only halfway work – but the psychological malnutrition also strikes me and is glaring. I assume that psychic nourishment of the expectant subject begins at best *in utero*, parallel to physical nourishment. The psychosomatic conditions *in utero* in the countries I am talking about here are clearly not building up the structures of the foetus in a supportive or even psychically enveloping way. Contrary to some ideas and fantasies about the seemingly dreamlike and childlike paradise-initiating nature of the African mother–baby relationship, which people from other continents attribute to African mothers and their babies partly because of the constant physical contact between baby and mother, I see quite different conditions. Malnourished, emaciated, overworked mothers, filled with the greatest worries about survival, who already have a great number of small children, always stillborn or dying soon after birth. Practically every woman knows the drama of the baby that she loses, that dies *in utero*, for example, and she does not know that this is a psychological drama, a traumatisation. She shrugs and says: that's just the way it is. At the same time, every new child is usually a burden because the mothers are also completely overburdened physically. They look after their children more or less – some grow up left behind, abandoned and try to earn

54 *The baby and the child without a mother*

money on their own in some way, often on the street or in big markets. And the husband takes often minimal, if any, care of his family, not even through work and/or with money, so as to feed his own family in the most rudimentary way. The children are there because God wants them, yet for the most part they are not wanted. Or if they are wanted, then possibly only in quantity, because in some African countries having a large number of children gives the mother a higher social standing. I have to describe this very bleak environment in a basic way so that my further reflections and clinical observations can be better understood.

When I work in the environment described above, I cannot assume – from a clinical point of view – that the inner processes alone determine the youngest children. Here, the environment plays an elementarily important role in the developmental process of the little ones, whether it is stimulating or destructive (Winnicott 1938) – probably a more important role than in many European areas. The early, mostly positive, fantasies attributed to European parents and their developing babies *in utero* cannot be considered ubiquitous. The process that develops from fertilisation in the child's mother is much more incidental in very poor and deprived social milieus and countries. Pregnancy often represents a nine-month period of life that the mother must "somehow" endure and "survive" in addition to the other burdens she carries. It is probably less about the conscious experience and the corresponding caring and joyful fantasies about the little one than about its and the mother's survival, if this is desired by the mother at all.

Sister and brother

I work briefly in an international organisation for orphans, which is under local management. The children are "shown" to me, in the afternoon, all together, during the break. I look at the balanced and at the same time lively break scene and start to "look in" a bit, to dream in. Now they immediately want to tell me something about the children. I ask to be allowed to look first, so that I can perhaps choose for myself which children I would like to work with individually. All of them are orphans who have often experienced terrible things. They were there when mother, father, siblings died, partly in war, partly because of HIV, partly because of hunger, thirst or because of domestic violence and/or abuse. While I am observing and noticing, they want to draw my attention to a girl who is strikingly very happy and jumping around. Unprompted and despite my request to be given no information, they tell me that she constantly wants to bite or bites her brother. Apparently, this act is so important that I absolutely have to be told about it. I have already noticed the brother: a decidedly classically beautiful boy, about 12 years old, skinny, showing the face of a cruel and rigid warrior, even and at the same time tense to the point of tearing or exploding. I say: "Yes, I mean the brother is probably not an easy member of the group either." "Exactly, he hits others and hits himself with others." Now I ask: "How is it with HIV, do they have children who are affected and do the children know this themselves?" "We can't talk about it," they answer, i.e. secretly they do have children who are affected, and the children themselves don't know. I now briefly report on my experiences with HIV-positive children and that, in my opinion, intuitively or preconsciously, they do know about their deadly disease. I only understand the deeper meaning of all this a little later.

Little A. tries to bite her brother T., initiating a fainting situation for the helpers. All the caregivers have to make sure that the two no longer fight together. But why? Arguing, fighting violently and also biting – these are common here in homes. Elsewhere, I had also been bitten, out of love-hate.

Back to the orphanage: once again I ask about HIV children. Yes, they tell me, but I shouldn't tell anyone, but I can tell you: "the little one who bites has AIDS and her brother doesn't." Now I am really horrified: a bite from the little one can bring death to her brother, who is healthy. She has realised how she can use her illness – of which she is aware – as a deadly weapon. Here the unconscious, the unconscious death wish for the rival brother is revealed unvarnished. And it also shows the new, the renewing aspect of my East African psychoanalytical work in the orphanages: I name connections that are not meant to be seen and that people are afraid of. I say that little A. can kill her brother and others with her biting. And she knows that, even if not entirely consciously.

Bibliography

Fanon, Frantz (1969). *The Wretched of the Earth*. New York: Grove Press (first edition 1961).

Freud, Sigmund (1905). *Drei Abhandlungen zur Sexualtheorie*. Leipzig and Wien: Franz Deuticke.

Freud, Sigmund (1920). *Jenseits des Lustprinzips*. Leipzig: Internationaler Psychoanalytischer Verlag.

Freud, Sigmund (1926). *Hemmung, Symptome und Angst*. Studienausgabe, vol. VI. Frankfurt am Main: Fischer.

Golse, Bernard and Roussillon, René (2015). *La naissance de l'objet. Une Co-construction entre le future sujet et ses objets à venir*. Paris: Humensis.

Green, André (2007). *Pourquoi les pulsions de destruction ou de mort?* Paris: Panama.

Green, André (2011). *Die tote Mutter. Psychoanalytische Studien zu Lebensnarzissmus und Todesnarzissmus*. Giessen: Psychosozial Verlag.

Spitz, René A. and Wolf, Katherine M. (1946). Anaclitic depression: an inquiry into the genesis of psychiatric conditions in early childhood, II. *The Psychoanalytic Study of the Child* 2(1): 313–342.

Winnicott, D. W. (1938). Shyness and nervous disorders in children. *The New Era in Home and School* 19(7): 189–191. Also published in *The Child and the Outside World: Studies in Developing Relationships*. London: Tavistock, 1957: pp. 35–39.

Ziegler, Jean (2016). *Der schmale Grat der Hoffnung: Meine gewonnenen und verlorenen Kämpfe und die, die wir gemeinsam gewinnen*. Munich: C. Bertelsmann.

56 *The baby and the child without a mother*

7 Babies with their mothers

My clinical experience in African orphanages and state hospitals, in a mostly extremely deprived milieu, shows me that the development of a defence against a part of the too-intrusive environmental impressions, i.e. life-threatening object influences, becomes effective very early in the unborn and in the baby, much earlier than psychoanalysts thought for a long time. It is possible that psychic defences, mainly dissociations, already begin prenatally, in the form of retarded development in the sense of a developmental standstill. I observe psychic self-movements such as the ones described. In the same rhythm as with the development of psychosomatic abilities and skills, the learning of how to configure and strengthen the narcissism of life, conversely the degradation of important cognitive, psychic, psychosomatic structures increases if there is no sufficiently nourishing (understood in the broadest sense of the word) environment. In the negative case, the little one crawls into the furthest corner of the small iron bed, literally crawls into itself and falls silent. The narcissism of death or the work of the drive of death reigns much earlier than is usually described. Whereas Spitz and Wolf (1946), with their concept of anaclitic depression, implicitly speak of such fatal withdrawal movements. If the object is not sufficiently good, this retreat into illness and into psychic and somatic dying begins.

Of all the orphanage and hospital babies in East African countries where I worked, 95% are physically extremely undernourished, for example completely dehydrated and malnourished, and consequently already ill at the time of their birth. The gastrointestinal tract and the respiratory tract only halfway work, and psychic malnutrition is also evident. I assume that psychic nourishment of the expectant subject begins at best *in utero*, parallel to physical nourishment. The psychosomatic conditions *in utero* in the countries I am working in are clearly not supportive or constructive for the structures of the foetus or even psychically enveloping. Contrary to some ideas and fantasies about the seemingly dreamlike and childlike paradise-initiating nature of the African mother–baby relationship, which some people from other continents attribute to African

DOI: 10.4324/9781003451587-7

58 *Babies with their mothers*

mothers and their babies partly because of the constant physical contact between baby and mother, I currently see quite different conditions: babies are born because God wants them, but I guess, for the most part they are not profoundly wanted by the mother. Or if they are wanted, then possibly only in the form of quantity, because in some East African countries, having a large number of children gives the mother a higher social standing.

I have to describe this somehow deprived and very sad environment in a basic way so that my further reflections and clinical observations can be better understood and the qualitative and quantitative differences in comparison with Western European situations become really clear.

When I work in the environment described above, I cannot assume, from a clinical point of view, that the inner processes alone determine the state of the youngest children. Here, the environment plays an elementarily important role in the developmental process of the little ones, whether it is stimulating or destructive (D. W. Winnicott 1940a, 1940b).

Probably it plays a more important role than in many European areas. The early, mostly positive, fantasies attributed to European parents and their developing babies *in utero* cannot be considered ubiquitous. The process that develops from fertilisation in the child's mother is much more incidental in very poor and deprived social milieus and countries. Pregnancy often represents a nine-month period of life that the mother must "somehow" endure and "survive" in addition to the other burdens she carries. It is probably less about the conscious experience and the corresponding caring and joyful fantasies about the little one, than about its and the mother's survival, if this is desired by the mother at all.

Vignettes

I describe here a psychoanalytic process in which I act psychoanalytically as an echo, as a double (Botella and Botella 2005), into the negative field (Green 2007) of the infant.

The lethargic boy in the big tent of Médecins Sans Frontières

In this clinical vignette, I describe my work with a boy of about five years of age, who has almost starved to death twice and whose body is covered with severe oedema. I am taken to Abu in a tent of Médecins Sans Frontières. He is very tall, completely lethargic, without tone, as if without muscles. He lies partly on top of or next to his mother, as if poured onto her, almost formless and completely passive. His hunger oedemas are in the foreground like signs of a terrible traumatisation and an approaching death. He does not allow himself to be addressed by me, nor to be touched psychologically. My kind of interventions, which usually prove successful in some African countries and homes and hospitals, do not seem to move him. His mother can hardly stand him, no, she basically rejects him, among other things, because he is always tearful and seems to take no notice of anyone, continuously whining and whimpering, and at the same time lying motionless half or completely poured over his mother's body. I feel exposed to many curious glances in this tent, and the little one probably does too. He seems to be on the way to dissolving, as it were, as a formless appendage of his mother and her body. In the tent, everyone hears his chronic whining and whimpering. I feel in myself the impulse (the mother's impulse?) to simply walk away, and have the feeling: it's hopeless. I feel helplessly exposed to this great visible misery, as if lost and at the same time under the most intense observation of the tent inhabitants, the other mothers and children, the relatives, the sceptical carers. Only the doctor has confidence in my work, but he is not present at the moment. After I decide not to run away and leave the tent, I start to echo him, repeating his wailing and moaning sounds for about 20 minutes. I pick up his whining and whimpering chant and echo it back. I feel absurd myself, especially in public, but I continue. It is about the little patient and not about me. And: it is extremely difficult to do this in his, Abu's, rhythm or non-rhythm, i.e. hopeless, tensionless, toneless, timeless, endless. Endless. I have to restrain myself from intoning ironically, or humorously, or encouragingly, or carelessly, or reproachfully, or acceleratingly, or aiming at a so-called goal, or too tearfully. I am beginning under pressure, paradoxically and unpleasantly, to be an adequate toneless echo to him. To be as much as possible a double to this endless whimpering lament, without wanting to change, without giving signs of not being able to endure. And I see no change in Abu's body-posture. I stop whiningly mirroring the moment I realise I can no longer go along as an echo, a moment that stretches as I realise I would now become inauthentic and acquiescent, like his mother, for example. And after that I remove myself from the tent.

The next day at noon, when I came back, the doctor said to me: Abu is sitting today – and he held out his hand for me to greet him. Up until now, he had been lying on this cot for months, exclusively powerless and miserable, and poured out on his mother. All this, in his passive activity of crying, whimpering, whining, singing.

This exchange surprises me very much. I am also amazed at how quickly something can be reorganised, when to a little one is given a good narcissistic occupation, that is bearable and nurturing to him. And: what happened clinically? What has straightened him up?

My attributed narcissistic affirmation and reinforcement in repetitive action, my purposelessness, my not pursuing a purpose – despite Abu's very dramatic psychosomatic situation, the fact of really staying in his rhythm and lament, concentrating on his narcissism completely, accepting him, taking him seriously, being a double to him. This may sound simple. But sometimes it was difficult for me not to let myself be displaced from his narcissism by

60   *Babies with their mothers*

inner impulses or by external ones from being a positive double in the negative field. I thought for moments I was crazy to do such a thing.

And finally, some reflections upon newborns and babies in African state hospitals.

The physical deformation of the newborn potentially begins with the genital mutilation of the little girl, most especially with the early deformation of her mother through third-stage –Pharaonic – genital mutilation, in all those countries in which I have worked.

The external somatic female mutilation also becomes an internal one, in a double sense. The natural orifices that allow urine and menstrual blood to flow out are, in the Pharaonic mutilation, sewn shut until they are only as big as a hazelnut. The little girl's legs are tied together after the mutilation, so that the wound grows together. The girl is thus immobilised at the same time after the procedure, she cannot run away, which would probably correspond to her impulse. She endures internal organic destruction and destruction on the border between inside and outside: fistulas, chronic cystitis, bladder incontinence, but of course also inner psychical injuries due to the trauma of the experience. Not to mention that the mutilation and sewing together of the vaginal opening are sometimes carried out in such a way that internal organs, such as a piece of the bladder or the kidney, are sewn together with the external seam that closes the genital opening and are thereby also destroyed, for example by being torn.

The baby in neonatology unable to drink

In neonatology, where I can work, thanks to my many years of African experience and learning from the baby and from the smallest ones in all the different orphanages, and thanks to my many years of clinical work as a psychoanalyst, the directing medical doctor brings a baby to me and says: "I don't know any more, I have to send the little one home. Without the feeding tube he will die. He has been hospitalised for seven days now and he is not getting better. His mother is there, but she can't breastfeed him, he won't do a thing."

Little Mh, seven days old, no longer shows any reflexes, no tone, his eyes are closed and he no longer reacts to anything. He looks as if he were dead. I begin my psychoanalytical work; I never know where it will lead. I try to satisfy his narcissism "all around", with my eyes and my other senses, but without touching him. In doing so, I start from my psychoanalytical inner frame: not being intrusive, seeing, hearing, smelling, waiting, calming to reinforce him and at the same time, in a triangulating function, creating a libidinous, a tendentially intrauterine space and container in which something can arise. I concentrate entirely on him, who no longer has any desire, and inwardly distance myself from the surroundings. (A large group of interested people is watching, because we work in a open court.) When I have an image of him, I touch his feet light as a feather, like a breath, and

Babies with their mothers 61

see if something happens and then form a kind of sole on the surface of his feet with my hands, which I make as soft as possible, like cotton wool. I give him a cotton floor, so to speak, for his feet and his psychosomatic body. Then I extend my touches over the whole foot and a little bit up over the heel. I talk to the little one, say his name, Mh, ask him in my mother tongue (Bernese dialect) about his life, explain his situation. I do all this in one and the same reassuring, not at all penetrating and at the same time vitalising tone of voice and I give rhythm, singsong and vocalisations (Maiello 1999). I undertake all this on the background of my psychoanalytic identity and my inner psychoanalytical frame. I do not push, I repeat myself rhythmically, I work as if time is not moving or running out and as if I had no sense of time. In this way I am close to my unconscious. I find myself in a kind of reverie of little Mh. At the same time, I offer myself, inactively, as a container in which perhaps something can unfold. I am in the paradoxical inner situation of a not-doing anything. And I repeat all these processes.

Suddenly, Mh opens his mouth a little, very, very slowly twists it into an attempt to smile, moves his feet a little, shows other reflexes, gets toned and opens his eyes and looks at me. And now, in my presence, he is present in his life and remains awake, interested and agile. Around me there are wondering and amazement at this newly awakened life. I continue to concentrate on the little one, talk to him, give him answers and enter into a calm and serene exchange with him. The medical director of the neonatal room immediately wants to put the baby to the mother's breast. I say no, "Later on, yes," because Mh has now done an enormous amount of work.

The colleague does not listen to me and after about half an hour brings the tiny Mh to his mother, who does not quite know what to do with him. Now I concentrate on the mother, who rather dislikes her little son because he takes up so much of her time – she already has many children at home – and of course also because he doesn't drink, which is a strong narcissistic mortification for her. I talk to her reassuringly, and much of our exchange happens non-verbally or in Bernese German and Somali at the same time. This mother, like most psychosomatically malnourished and genitally mutilated African mothers I have worked with, is in desperate need of psycho-narcissistic nourishment. During this time of more or less verbal exchange, I tenderly stroke Mh's mother's back. This is indispensably important for her own body feeling to change and for new psychosomatic processes to be set in motion. I talk to her tenderly and quietly, as if she were the baby. Apart from the many traumas and the great lack she experiences in many respects, jealousy of the little one, who seems to receive a heavenly amount of attention from me, surely also plays a role for the mother. In any case, Mh's mother manages to take him in her arms, in a different way now, more softly, and to look at him. And finally, Mh begins to look and suck very hesitantly. And his mother looks at me. Now she probably accepts him enough so that he can survive.

62   *Babies with their mothers*

What happens between the baby, the traumatised mother and me when such transformations of gradual dissolution into nirvana – probably in the environment of the death drive (Freud 1920) – and re-forming in the environment of the life drive happen?

My containing seems to be able to procure the base of a potential space for self-movement and self-development in babies, infants, pregnant women and mothers who are subjected to various traumatising situations that are difficult to endure. In my experience, this is hardly known in African orphanages and hospitals – and probably only partially also in European ones. As a rule, the focus is understandably on the cases where somatic survival encounters extreme difficulties.

What further psychoanalytical considerations can be linked to my clinical work, especially my work with Mh?

Golse says that psychic processes are already ongoing in a baby at the time of its birth, and these increase in complexity over time. In this way, only if one assumes the foetus begins to experience a psychic life prenatally is psychic transgenerational transmission logically possible.

I make use of the five senses and also make conscious and intensive use of the sonorous. The prenatal baby is the only part-object that hears its mother's voice from inside and outside (Braconnier and Golse 2010; Maiello 2012).

D. Houzel (in Pestalozzi et al. 1998) writes:

The newborn is in possession of psychic parts that are already born, and parts that are not yet born. The yet unborn parts of the infant's psychism are probably those that have not yet been able to be contained by the thoughts of, most likely, the mother, while the born parts of the psychism have already been contained by the thoughts of another.

This being thought through another in order to be able to unfold is, as I already mentioned, hardly typical for African conditions.

In my work I also become this Other who contains and translates back certain parts of the psychism of the small and the big. I often work with babies, very small children and adults along a borderline, on a fine line that decides whether they give up all desire, remain in passivation (André Green 2007, 2011) and withdraw into the realm of the death instinct or whether I can interest them in an exchange in a uterus-like psychosomatic climate. In doing so, I experience how quickly interest and desire can come alive again if there is only one object that brings full narcissistic occupation, i.e. a psycho-economic balance, and becomes a double for a short time (René Roussillon 2008).

It seems important to me to receive the psychic, often very small signs of coming alive in exchange – one patient only stretched a little finger in my direction – of the other person in my containing and to acknowledge this

Babies with their mothers 63

affirmatively or to react and signal back that their signs are perceived and can develop further and further. In other words, I make them understand that a reciprocal space is there and connects us, by means of their signs, which I integrate into mine and in turn convey back to them as ours.

All this just mentioned culminates in the risky touching of the so extremely fragile premature babies, the smallest and the endangered one, panic-stricken pregnant women and women giving birth. Can the smallest and the largest bear what is being done to them? Does it calm down a little? Does it become more alive? This psychosomatic exchange, the circularity of the encounter, is not a manipulation that would be limited to doing something to the other. I adapt my psychoanalytic action as far as possible in the right timing to the smallest existing physical expressions of the small and larger other.

I am not aiming at anything but am in a dreamy state, am concentrated and at the same time not concentrated, and perceive what is happening or arising. I have no guiding or determining function. I do not want anything. I do and do not do anything purposeful at the same time. This seems simple, but it is one of the most difficult things in working with newborns who are slowly approaching death. People want to put pressure on you – "orient yourself to the machines about you to ensure the success and progress of your work," they tell me. This is one of the points that differentiates my work from some sort of medicine.

Thus, at best, a new, or rather a rediscovered form of the nurturing psychosomatic exchange that takes place *in utero* configures itself. A representation of the nurturing exchange with an Other emerges, which is not too much an Other, but always also a good enough double. The small and the large can thus construct within themselves the representation of a reciprocal object-relationship that is worth seeking and seeking again. Desire does not quite die and so the narcissism of life, the vitality of the baby, infant and pregnant woman, does not die either, because a mental survival optic has now been formed. And desire does not quite die, and desire can desire, even if quietly.

Bibliography

Bion, W. R. (2005a). *The Tavistock Seminars*. London: Karnac Books. (German ed.: *Die Tavistock-Seminare*. Frankfurt am Main: Brandes & Apsel, 2007.)

Bion, W. R. (2005b). *The Italian Seminars*. London: Karnac Books. (German ed.: *Die italienischen Seminare*. Frankfurt am Main: Brandes & Apsel, 2007.)

Botella, Sára and Botella, César (2005). *The Work of Psychic Figurability: Mental States Without Representation*. London: Routledge.

Braconnier, A. and Golse, B. (2010). *Dépression du bébé, dépression de l'adolescent* (Le Carnet psy). Toulouse: éditions érès.

Freud, Sigmund (1920). *Jenseits des Lustprinzips*. Leipzig: Internationaler Psychoanalytischer Verlag.

Green, André (2007). *Pourquoi les pulsions de destruction ou de mort?* Paris: Panama.

64 *Babies with their mothers*

Green, André (2011). *Die tote Mutter. Psychoanalytische Studien zu Lebensnarzissmus und Todesnarzissmus*. Giessen: Psychosozial Verlag.

Hirsi Ali, A. (2015). *Reformiert euch! Warum der Islam sich ändern muss*. München: Knaus.

Leiris, Michel (1985). *Phantom Afrika. Tagebuch einer Expedition von Dakar nach Dschibuti 1931–1933*. First and second parts. Introduction by Hans-Jürgen Heinrichs. Trans. by Rolf Wintermeyer. Frankfurt am Main: Suhrkamp.

Maiello, Suzanne (1999). Das Klangobjekt. Über den pränatalen Ursprung auditiver Gedächtnisspuren. *Psyche – Zeitschrift für Psychoanalyse* 53B(2): 137–157.

Maiello, S. (2012). Prenatal experiences of containment in the light of Bion's model of container/contained. *Journal of Child Psychotherapy* 38(3): 250–267.

Özdaglar, Aydan (2016). *Psychoanalytische Autorität in der Arbeit mit Patienten aus dem muslimischen Kulturkreis*. European Psychoanalytical Federation Conference, Berlin, 17–20 March 2016.

Pestalozzi, J., Frisch, S., Hinshelwood, R. D. and Houzel, D. (Eds.). (1998). *Psychoanalytic Psychotherapy in Institutional Settings*. London: Routledge.

Racamier, Paul-Claude (1993). *Le Psychanalyste sans divan. La psychanalyse et les institutions de soins psychiatriques*. Bibliothèque Scientifique Payot. Paris: Payot.

Roussillon, René (2008). *Le jeu et l'entre-je(u)*. Paris: Presses Universitaires de France.

Saegesser, Barbara (2012). *Meine psychoanalytische Arbeit in verschiedenen afrikanischen Ländern*. Basel: Vortrag Psychoanalytisches Seminar.

Saegesser, Barbara (2014). Psychoanalytische Arbeit mit BB's, Kleinkindern und Müttern in unterschiedlichen afrikanischen Ländern (Le travail psychanalytique avec les bébés, des petits enfants et des mères dans divers pays d'Afrique). *Schweizerische Gesellschaft für Psychoanalyse – SGPsa Bulletin* No. 77 (Spring): 5–13.

Saegesser, Barbara (2015). Psychoanalytische Feldarbeit in ostafrikanischen Städten. In: Peter Bründl and Carl E. Scheidt (Eds.), *Spätadoleszenz. Identitätsprozesse und kultureller Wandel. Jahrbuch der Kinder- und Jugendlichen Psychoanalyse*, vol. 4. Frankfurt am Main: Brandes & Apsel: pp. 212–239.

Saegesser, Barbara (2016a). Elternschaft in ostafrikanischen Städten. Psychoanalytische Arbeit mit Müttern, Ersatzmüttern, Vätern und Waisenkindern. In: P. Bründl, M. Endres, and H. Hauser (Eds.), *Elternschaft: klinische und entwicklungspsychologische Perspektiven. Jahrbuch der Kinder- und Jugendspezifischen-Psychoanalyse*, vol. 5. Frankfurt am Main: Brandes & Apsel: pp. 269–285.

Saegesser, Barbara (2016b). Un travail psychothérapeutique en marge de ma pratique psychoanalytique et de la culture islamique dans des villes d'Afrique de l'est. (Translation and adaptation of my original manuscript written in German.) *Tribune Psychanalytique* 13.

Saegesser, Barbara (2016c). Eine Skizze psychoanalytischer Arbeit in ostafrikanischen islamischen Städten. Islamische religiös-weltliche Gesetze und Normen als Basis für Widerstand und Abwehrbewegungen von PatientInnen im Rahmen (situativ angepasster) psychoanalytischer Arbeit. *„A jour"*, 2.

Saegesser, Barbara (2017). „Gleichschwebende" Assessments, ambulatorisches Auswählen und psychoanalytische Kurzpsychotherapie mit adoleszenten Patientinnen im ostafrikanischen Krankensaal. In: Peter Bründl and Fernanda Pedrina (Eds.). *Abklärung – Diagnose – Fallbeschreibung, Forschung und Behandlungsplan. Jahrbuch der Kinder- und Jugendlichen-Psychoanalyse*, vol. 6. Frankfurt am Main: Brandes & Apsel: pp. 196–215.

Spitz, René A. (1946). Hospitalism: a follow-up report on investigation described in volume I, 1945. *The Psychoanalytic Study of the Child* 2(1): 113–117.

Spitz, René A. and Wolf, Katherine M. (1946). Anaclitic depression: an inquiry into the genesis of psychiatric conditions in early childhood, II. *The Psychoanalytic Study of the Child* 2(1): 313–342.

Winnicott, D. W. (1940a). Children and their mothers. *The New Era in Home and School* 21. Republished in L. Caldwell and H. T. Robinson (Eds.), *The Collected Works of D. W. Winnicott: Volume 2, 1939–1945*. Oxford: Oxford University Press, 2016: pp. 81–86.

Winnicott, D. W. (1940b). The deprived mother [1939]. *The New Era in Home and School* 21(3). Republished in L. Caldwell and H. T. Robinson (Eds.), *The Collected Works of D. W. Winnicott: Volume 2, 1939–1945*. Oxford: Oxford University Press, 2016: pp. 35–42.

8   Sex/gender differences

The "surgically" manipulated and changed female genital field

In the East African areas where I work, and which I try to get to know and understand psychoanalytically and from cultural-religious, political and ethnological viewpoints, psychotherapy for children and adults was, even in large cities, until recently almost entirely unavailable, if known at all. The legislative template for thought and action in these regions is the Quran with its various Hadiths (appendices) and interpretations. The Quran implies that independent critical thinking and feeling are to be discouraged. What is expected instead is complete devotion and orientation towards the Quran and Quranic verse. Consequently, no processes are in place that facilitate the development of self-recognition, the protection and strengthening of the self, and the search for ego-authenticity through, for example, psychotherapeutic or psychoanalytic work.

I have – as a novelty, in an East African environment – carried out psychoanalytic and psychotherapeutic work there (see Saegesser 2015, 2016a, 2017, 2018).

In Western Africa (especially Senegal), and possibly also in certain regions of North and Southern Africa, the situation in this regard is different. From these parts of the continent, which seem more open to Western European concepts and ways of thinking, there are reports of psychotherapies being carried out with children as well as adults.

The reasons for this lack of psychotherapeutic and psychoanalytic work in East Africa are manifold. At the centre is, I believe, the strict, as if by law adherence to the Quranic commandments and regime, which in its interpretation opposes most tendencies towards individualisation in the believer.

The population in East Africa, the Bantus, adhere, as a rule, to family traditions and to their own political-religious cultural conventions that count like laws, which secure family ties and family cohesion far beyond the national borders that were artificially imposed on the continent by the former colonial powers. Many children are born into strict Quranic family traditions and ways of life. These ancient laws and regulations, supported

DOI: 10.4324/9781003451587-8

by the Quran, the family traditions and the family holding together overall across all fixed borders, the so-called Umma, also include the tradition that one's own and adopted children can be passed on to other branches of the extended family, if a family becomes too large in number, or where family members and children start to cause difficulties. These children are, for example, shipped from an island to the mainland, or sent from one country to another, far-off region. This is undertaken without the possibility of daily phone calls home, or keeping in contact via chats online, as would be the case, for example, in Europe. The money for such facilities is simply not there. These transfers put very real, geographical distances between the children and their families, something which happens especially also in those family situations where children begin to be "difficult" as a result of being caught up in the process of a familial conflict. It is probably the sort of moment at which Western European children would often be referred to psychotherapy. In especially severe cases of mental problems, and where such problems are regarded as caused by evil spirits (as defined by the Quran), people in East African urban areas tend to seek advice from healers and healing through traditional medicinal cures – in this case only modest amounts of money are involved. Healers in mostly all-African regions rely for their craft on oral tradition, ancient rituals and frequently also herbal cures (Saegesser 2018).

A major part of the population in East Africa orientates themselves to some extent by what they know from the Quran, by what they have heard about it as children, and what they have learnt off by heart at the madrasas, the traditional children's educational establishments of the region. All this, they would experience in the language of High Arabic, as a result of which the deeper meaning of their religious templates and guidelines probably largely escapes them. The parts of the Quran with which people are generally familiar are the suras, short passages or succinct sayings from the Quran. A prerequisite to being able to read and understand the original version of the Quran is an excellent knowledge of High Arabic. This, however, is not taught at schools. Presumably, mastering High Arabic and reading texts from the Quran in their original version is deemed the exclusive preserve of some people of the higher social classes and the inner religious circle. Much of the Quran's contents consist of the Hadiths: a body of collected texts which were added to the Quran to supplement it and to interpret its teachings. These texts contain laws, regulations and directions that were recorded and translated by their original recorders and, as such, reflect the thoughts and interpretations of these recorders. In principle, the texts are said to be the Prophet Mohammed's thoughts and teachings. Mohammed, in turn, ascribes them to Allah. The various contents of the Hadiths have over the centuries either been challenged by important personages such as the Khalifs or were considered indisputably authoritative and therefore written into Islamic law.

68 *Sex/gender differences*

Malise Ruthven (2010) summarises in the following terms. Since the Quran's beginnings, many uncertainties have arisen and countless alterations have been made to it, but the central question is, whether it is the Prophet's teachings that count, or the teachings of the Hadiths; or, whether it is what the Khalifs at a particular time say, who, depending on the status of power they hold, would have the legal authority to make amendments to the original texts and sayings.

Nowadays, there appear to be radical differences in the various interpretations of Quranic law, causing serious rifts among different groups such as the Sunnites and Shiites.

The Quran is a **code of law** and not a guide to Muslim life, as, for example, the Bible is to Christian life. The role of the Imam, or priest of Islam, is not to teach how to be a devout Muslim. An Imam is tasked with the protection of the law and the most important rules and regulations. There is, e.g. Sharia law, and there is Sunna law. When the last, final regulation or decision is pronounced, this will be, viewed objectively, the result of a logical reasoning process. If there are no rules or regulations available for a particular set of circumstances, case precedent comes into play: the actual problem is discussed in depth, based on similar previous examples, then an answer is found by logical deduction and reasoning.

And in principle, writes Malise Ruthven, many of the commandments contained in the Quran are ambiguously worded in such a way that they remain wide open to interpretation. It is particularly also this contradictory nature of the formulations of these laws that lies at the heart of many past and current conflicts between the various Islamic groups and factions, as already indicated.

Based on my assumption and my personal experience of the region that all East African thinking, behaviour and experience are oriented towards Quranic law and order, I started to search in the Quran for information about its position regarding gender differences between boys and girls.[1] While I found many instances of text passages declaring that boys and girls must be treated equally, I did not find any parts stating clearly that boys and girls, although differing from each other in their respective genders, are equal in society and before the law and, presumably, before Allah. I did find one statement, however, that proclaims that both men and women should accumulate as much knowledge as possible. The Quran is an enormously difficult text to read – it is complex and extremely densely written. I rely on Quran specialists who cite and interpret selected passages from it. One commentator writes on how the Quran condemns in the strongest terms the gruesome practice of burying newborn female babies in the sand alive. And as for the tradition of slaughtering two sheep on the birth of a boy and one sheep only on the birth of a girl, the Quran appears to condemn this ritual, too, and to suggest that this be changed. The fact that the Quran addresses gender equality and, in this connection, implicitly calls for change in respect of certain traditional practices and behaviours, leads to the suspicion that the everyday reality of attitudes towards and the handling of gender-related issues may look somewhat different.

The female gender and its significance in society, and the discourse (in the broadest sense) with and about it, are, in comparison with those of the male, tinged with negative and degrading attributes and connotations and actions against women. Boys and girls are not equal. The birth of a boy is, for the father, of enormous significance and, indirectly, on account of this, also to the mother. She is valuable to her husband if she gives birth to a son, just as if she alone had determined the sex of the child. The value of the woman is not intrinsic to her sex – it is attributed to her by her husband on account of the value she confers on him as his virgin woman, her virginity being a fact that he will likely have made public. And this value (or non-value) assignment begins immediately at birth, right at the very start of a male or a female human life.

For proof of this, especially in the geographic regions where I work, I can rely relatively safely on my own everyday observations that I make of the social and familial treatment of girls and boys. The imbalance in the treatment of boys and girls is clearly reflective of the difference in value society attaches to either boys or girls. This sprang out at me on my first visit to an orphanage, where such difference in treatment became clearly evident in the types of furniture in the girls' and boys' rooms. Next to each boy's bed stood a small wooden cupboard. Next to each girl's bed lay a plastic bag, for them to put their clothes in. It is similar in hospitals: men in men's rooms tend to lie in modern, height-adjustable beds. Women do not.

Out in the streets, I hardly ever meet a girl alone. Boys, however, are everywhere. Women almost never visit here – it is boys and men who populate the centre of town and the restaurants, where they sit and drink their tea and play together.

In most scriptures, the circumcisions of boys and girls are mentioned in one and the same statement – as if they were analogous. The two cutting procedures involved are, however, entirely and completely different in reality. The boy undergoes circumcision: a relatively safe, hygienic, medically based procedure. This is subsequently celebrated extensively in the company of family and guests.

By contrast, the so-named (which is incorrect) "circumcision" of a girl is female genital mutilation, and happens in secret and entails serious negative consequences: heavy loss of blood; legs tightly bound together for a period of around four weeks; unspeakable physical pain; mostly lifelong chronic illness. This invasive – in both somatic and psychic reality – procedure, resulting in the brutal destruction of the female sex anatomy, can be understood symbolically, psychoanalytically, and in a psycho-somatic way. It bears testimony to the actual, real, incisive difference between the sexes/genders in (not only) East Africa. The concept and project of hurting and destructing women in a terrible way is found in

70   Sex/gender differences

the Quran. There are hints and directions of what a man should do with an unwilling and rebellious woman, how to chastise and punish her: he should punish her so that she becomes truly subservient to him, and so on. If he physically beats her, he should do so in a way that leaves no traces visible to the outside world. This, indeed, is not only written and projected but physically put into practice in the extreme with the procedure of female genital mutilation.

If I bring Freud into play in this connection, I conclude that, in East African regions, a female anatomy is not fate but a severely mutilated and fundamentally destroyed female sex landscape.

As far as I am aware, the definition and implication of sex differences per se hardly seem to play a role in general discourse in East Africa. In East African regions, the actual, real sex/gender difference, not the theoretical, projected one, is being physically lived by more than 50% of women and girls who have been genitally mutilated. They do so in painful obscurity, their achiness hidden under long clothes, and, when engaged in social activities, they veiled and disguised their shame.

The Quran correspondingly stipulates a certain form of dress code: the dignity of the woman should be esteemed and preserved to the same extent as that of the man. The prescription of suitable types of clothes that serve to preserve this dignity applies equally to both men and women. Muslim dress should veil the believers to such an extent that the wearer neither evokes nor elicits the interest of the opposite sex. Women, in addition, are directed to wear the hijab (veil or headscarf) to cover their hair, since the sight of female hair is considered especially seductive and titillating.

The actual manipulated gender differences appear brutally clearly defined, especially against the background of the fact that the biological female condition is, through an imposed physical intervention, actively being altered and destroyed. Misogyny is in action, pure and simple. I witness this gender difference on the maternity wards where I work. I watch, listen and call out these brutal acts that symbolically express a society's profound desire to decimate the female potential and to create a massive gender difference through actual physical destruction and mutilation. As a European woman in East Africa, I am in the unique position of being able to challenge, question and personally condemn these atrocious rituals and customs. In everyday life in East Africa, the topic is beyond the bounds of public discourse. Those who are oblivious of the desperate misery that was inflicted on girls and women in the past, and is still being inflicted now, will remain so. They will notice nothing.

In actual fact, the female inner space – with the exception of the space of the womb – and the female capability of experiencing sexual pleasure, are destroyed. Fantasising, thinking and attributions are not enough in this cultural, religious and political environment. A "passage à l'acte" (the enacting or living out of a fantasy) takes its course. The misogyny is being acted out, the true nature of the female biology and physicality denied or

Sex/gender differences 71

rejected and, in psychoanalytic terms, the psychotic desire to really destructively physically aggress and sometimes kill the girl/woman, at least to castrate her, is made real.

The sexual organs and sexuality play (compared to Freudian sexual theory and subsequent, much later, theory of female analysts), on the one hand, for these women, a lesser role as an object for seeking pleasure than for men. Whereas, the boys – and this puts them back in a prominent role – are, unlike in many other cultures, cut (circumcision) a few days after birth. This has got medical justifications as well as happening for the reason to make men's sexual pleasure more intense. In East African cities, from Alexandria to the Indian Ocean, the act named circumcision, being in reality a genital mutilation, with girls is 100% different. The name "Pharaonica" is given to the most extreme form of genital mutilation: the inner and outer labia are cut away, the clitoris is cut away and the vaginal opening is stitched together to the point where only a small opening the size of a hazelnut (1–2 cm) remains for urine and blood to pass through. The inner space, the inner genital space, the significance of which, as has been emphasised especially by women psychoanalysts, is all-important for the essence of the female being, is prevented from playing a central role for the woman. For the woman, sexual pleasure must not play a role, but it must do so for the man, who penetrates her and for whom the vaginal opening has been made especially small to put male pleasure and, in most cases, female pain at the centre of the sexual act. The outer and inner female sexual organs are being destroyed so that the woman can no longer experience sexual pleasure – most women suffer extremely during the sexual activity of their men – while the sexual pleasure of the man is, on account also of the sensitivity of the head of his penis, considerably enhanced.

Both genders are circumcised, but in markedly different ways and for different reasons. When both acts are mentioned together, the actual terror of the female circumcision, the effective genital mutilation inflicted on girls, is never articulated – except when it is "only" the outer labia that is being removed, which is then equated as a little bit similar to the "slightly superfluous loose skin" that is cut away in the circumcision of a boy. Even official national or international organisations fail to specify the finer details of the horror, namely, that girls are, for no valid medical reason but based on tradition (from ancient Egypt) and religious beliefs, outwardly as well as inwardly crudely mutilated, and only this hazelnut-sized opening is left open for urine and menstrual blood to pass through. For the equally gruesome act of the suturing of the wound, the medical term "infibulation" is frequently applied – a term that most people do not really understand, and which completely obfuscates the true nature of what it designates. It is an act done by persons – often the mother – that have no idea about the female body and cutting in the female body. And they do not use a real cutting knife. Another detail that is hardly ever mentioned in official communiqués is the fact that this

72 Sex/gender differences

mutilating "operation" has lifelong serious health consequences for girls, and later women. Most mutilated women suffer excruciating pain during sexual intercourse and while giving birth. At the point of giving birth, the mutilated and heavily scarred, hardened tissue comes negatively into play, tissue that would normally have a soft, natural flexibility, especially so in the pregnant female body that prepares itself for the impending act of birthing. The female inner space and the canal leading to the outside world, the birth canal, are both hardened by mutilation. Besides the extreme pain experienced by the mother, this has adverse effects also for the baby about to be born. Especially the little head will be more than normally squashed and crushed to the point where small brain lesions can often result. In East African hospitals, if surgical facilities are available, and for the reasons just described, medical (here in the real medical sense) caesarean sections are performed if the mother's life is considered to be in danger. In these regions, the statistical norm for caesarean deliveries lies above the African norm. But their religion forbids caesarean sections. This is true in cities from the north, e.g. Alexandria, to the Indian Ocean. The choice of a caesarean delivery cannot be decided by the doctors or by the birthing mother herself. Her man or her father must be asked. She has no say in this. If neither her father nor her husband can be found in time, this may, in some cases, mean certain death for her. No medical doctor dares to intervene without having secured the husband or father's authority first. By performing caesarean sections, doctors are doing an act in contravention of the Quran. On many occasions, it is left to me to negotiate with husbands or fathers in favour of a birthing woman, whose life is completely in danger of death without caesarean section. Nobody enjoys having to conduct such negotiations, and it takes considerable courage and fortitude to do so and to stand one's ground when trying to win over a man of Muslim faith who finds himself in a situation which is developing in a direction away from Quranic conformity. Especially foreign doctors find themselves in disbelief, frustration and despair in such situations.

My reasons for going into such detail in my description of these often-life-threatening situations in which expectant mothers find themselves when giving birth, are that I wish to illustrate how, in this context, too, in this whole medical-political religious process and procedure, the immense, through the direct mutilation effected, destruction of the female sex landscape prominently comes to the fore once again, and leads near to death for the pregnant woman now, as it did before with her life as a girl in the moment of her early mutilation.

Both in what I have just described and in what I shall describe in what follows, I write in frank, candid and unadorned terms about all these atrocities committed for the sake of an artificially created female sex, these acts of female genital mutilation (FGM). In doing so, I have also chosen not to give special consideration to the feelings of my readers. The issue at hand is too important, and it is my belief that it is crucial to learn in detail the full, heavy facts as they really are. I hope my readers will recognise with me the need for these desperate situations to be exposed to the full light of public thinking and emotions, even though it may be shocking and painful to read.

In fundamental contrast to boys, sickness is purposely brought upon girls. Not only sickness, but humiliation too. I work and move in countries that practise maximal degrees of genital circumcision and genital mutilation: in Ethiopia, Sudan, Djibouti and in parts of Tanzania with refugees from Eritrea and Somalia. In all these countries, the incident rate of FGM amongst girls is higher than 50%. Their mutilation starts shortly after birth and continues through to the ages of around 12–15.

For the girls, FGM has both physical (see above) as well as mental consequences such as a traumatic fear of being physically approached, especially sexually, serious depressive reactions, deep feelings of shame accompanied by states of purposelessness, emptiness and passivity – and all this often on a lifelong basis. The procedures are usually carried out without anaesthetic and with crude, unsterilised cutting tools such as shards of earthenware or glass, or with razor blades. The potential for infection is enormous. The pain the girls are subjected to during the procedure is unimaginable, inhumane; the wounds bleed excessively; many pass out or end up in severe shock. Some subsequently die from, for example, bleeding to death.

Today there are surgeons (e.g. in Djibouti or the Kivu region of the Democratic Republic of the Congo) who specialise in operating on women whose bladder, kidneys or large intestine were injured during the so-called circumcision procedure or are caught up in the stitches of the genital wounds. Generally, mutilated women are, for understandable reasons, afraid of physical contact or manipulation in the lower regions of their bodies, especially so before operations or before giving birth, and there is a danger that they may be re-traumatised after surgical intervention.

Even though in many countries FGM is now banned, estimates suggest that there are around 200 million genitally mutilated women in the world today. If men and women are asked why this might be so, they say, according to surveys from the countries concerned: because it's accepted practice. People refuse to look closely. Or, if the question is put to well-educated Muslims, they counter, in a poorly veiled attempt to avoid the actual reality, that genital mutilation had originally nothing to do with Quranic teachings; that it was once a ritual taken over from Egypt in the past, with the aim of delighting and satisfying the Egyptian Nile god with the labia of virgins.

Psychoanalytically speaking, with all these restricting, degrading, confining, physically mutilating, and castrating social acts against the woman, sanctioned by religious, political, cultural and tradition-based conventions, and taking into account also the unconscious level of awareness, it appears, in a psychoanalytical view, as if in the unconscious, in the Dark

74 *Sex/gender differences*

Continent, the women were holding the status of an all-powerful being like, for example, the omnipotent mother in the description and conceptualisation by Janine Chasseguet-Smirgel (1970, 1986); or the mother, in whose womb orgiastic feasts are held after the concept of Melanie Klein (1962, 1987); or, maybe, the woman that gave, somehow, birth to Christian human descendants, Holy Mary, who, in East Africa, takes the name of Mariam and there is a quite important form of the cult of Mariam. The radius of influence of these fantasised and experienced images of the omnipotent woman, and the fatal jealousy growing from them, along with the fear and horror this jealousy engenders, might, in a phantasmatic way, be seen or understood to curtail the largely unlimited power of the man, partially the power of the Prophet and possibly even the omnipotence of God. This terrible, fantasised catastrophe for the male gender must be prevented at all costs, namely through the – seemingly psychotic – act of the thorough and complete destruction of the female biological sex and ability to experience pleasure, to be fertile without problems, to engender the future and to ensure the continuation of mankind.

With this newly, artificially "created", i.e. destructive, gender difference engineered by mutilating the female sex based on a concept moulded from thought and fantasy into horrific reality, and by physically entirely deviating from the natural anatomy, the ultimate degradation of the female is "surgically" brought to completion.

The girl's mother is evidently the driving force behind the genital mutilation of her daughter, and her motivation seems to be the following: I am of the Islamic tradition and remain faithful to it and would never interrupt this mutilating series of physical torture. I have no other choice. You, as my daughter, must remain in the same tradition, and you shall have it neither differently nor better than I did, and still do. The extended family – within the framework of the Umma – and the neighbours shall be satisfied with us, which will lead to a harmonious coexistence between us. The developmental fate of the daughter is, seen in this way, closely tied to that of her mother. The girl's development runs along pre-oedipal tracks as a duplication of the mother's anatomical and psychic fate. It seems to me that a form of concentrated hatred builds up in the mother, expressly because of her fate as a genitally mutilated, permanently controlled, and subservient woman. And the mother succeeds in her somewhat psychotic, intrusive living-out of this hatred through the genital mutilation of her daughter. The active mother will harbour fears of retribution, and the daughter possibly unconscious fantasies of revenge and unlived wishes for retaliation. After all the suffering the girl has been subjected to by her mother, she will continue to live and grow up in the custody of that mother, who remains forever conscious of her own destructed sexuality. The girl will be watched and supervised closely, as many young women are (Hirsi Ali 2015), since, in many Muslim families, entering marriage as a virgin is still the highest distinction to strive for.

Sex/gender differences 75

The destructive, mutilating act of FGM, often executed by the mother in collaboration with a female aide, transforms the girl, according to Quranic law, into a woman. From then on – in the broadest sense – the girl can be married off and thus achieve the most desirable social goal: becoming the wife of a man. Only as the wife of a man does the East African woman become a human being that deserves some measure of attention and a quantum of respect.

I cannot comment much on the oedipal development of boys and the corresponding conflicts. It is certain that, in principle, the boy enjoys a closer relationship with his father, especially also on account of the father's pride in his son, that is, he takes great pride in "having one". The son is considered "the son of the father" and may, as a result, to some extent suffer from diminished self-esteem (in name, he remains the son of . . .). With girls, probably on account of the inferior status attributed to them, the situation is different.

By my observations and contacts, I am able to explore in an indirect way, rather than in a direct way where I would have to ask direct questions. I believe that there are certain problems concerning women that, although pressing, cannot be discussed openly with others. Addressing such problems would be fully deemed unseemly, very unwelcome, and put me vis-à-vis others in an awkward position, resulting in no more than vague replies. I would also be challenging people – women – to think for themselves, and this does not come naturally in an environment like theirs because, for almost all life situations, including for how to think, the Quran provides rules, directives and laws to follow. I have encountered a small number of exceptions: a conversation with a vastly experienced, older, intelligent and witty, partly traditionally trained midwife. She offered me important insights which helped me to understand in more detail the kind of suffering the women themselves would never reveal or talk about. She told me of marriages of young girls to, in this region (Somalia), extremely old-seeming men (13- to 14-year-olds to 60-year olds), and the unusual sexual practices which are said to favour the eventual birth of a boy; about the excruciating physical pain genitally mutilated birthing mothers go through during the whole birthing process up until the point when the baby's little head makes contact with her perineum, which had been sewn up along with her entire mutilated external genitals (barring that tiny hazelnut-sized opening described earlier). I have witnessed such appalling situations myself while assisting in the delivery room. The midwife also told me of physical traces of the serious abuse some of these women suffer at the hands not only of their husbands but also, especially in the northeastern parts of Africa (frequently Egypt), of their mothers-in-law, such as scald marks caused by hot oil, injuries caused by poisonous substances and so on.

Other direct, lifelong effects of "surgical" interventions performed on the girls by mothers, aunts or specialised female mutilationists include: illnesses such as AIDS, blood poisoning and tetanus through the use of unclean "surgical" instruments.

76 *Sex/gender differences*

At a psychological level, depression, severe anxieties and, of course, the psychosomatic syndromes of a heavily traumatised human being are to be expected throughout the rest of their lives.

The East African Muslim sex/gender difference cannot, in the sense described, be subjected to nuanced and systematic comparison with Western psychoanalytic, psychological and physical developmental lines. The position of the East African girl, and later woman, is, in a Quran-oriented society, different from the position of the girl and woman in Western European societies. And yet, societal attitudes to women on both continents show, to differing extents, a tendency to degrade the female, or to actively put into practice such degradation. And in both societies, East African as well as Western European, there are continued calls for improvement in accepting girls (women) and boys (men) as equal human beings in society, in their daily work to get money and before the law, and for efforts to be undertaken accordingly in order to realise this aim.

Note

1 The German expression "Gender" is to be understood in a biological-sexual way, without connection to the society. This marks a difference to the English expression of Gender, which is connected also to social meanings. The German words Sex and Gender are to be regarded as descriptions of two different meanings and designating the very facts as independent from one another.

Bibliography

Chasseguet-Smirgel, Janine (1970). *Female Sexuality: New Psychoanalytic Views*. London: Routledge.

Chasseguet-Smirgel, Janine (1986). *Sexuality and Mind: The Role of the Father and Mother in the Psyche*. London: Routledge.

Erikson, E. H. (1974). Weiblichkeit und der innere Raum. In: *Jugend und Krise*. Stuttgart: Klett-Cotta: pp. 274–308.

Freud, Sigmund (1920). *Jenseits des Lustprinzips*. Studienausgabe, vol. III. Frankfurt am Main: Fischer.

Freud, Sigmund (1926). *Hemmung, Symptom und Angst*. Studienausgabe, vol. VI. Frankfurt am Main: Fischer.

Grifel, Frank (2018). *Den Islam denken*. Stuttgart: Reclam.

Hanneman, Isabelle (2013). Über das Dunkle im dunklen Kontinent. Leerstellen im Konstrukt weiblicher Identität. *Psychologie und Gesellschaftskritik* 36/37(4/I): 125–149.

Hirsi Ali, A. (2015). *Reformiert euch! Warum der Islam sich ändern muss*. München: Knaus.

Klein, Melanie (1962). Neid und Dankbarkeit. In: *Das Seelenleben des Kleinkindes und andere Beiträge zur Psychoanalyse*. Stuttgart: Klett: pp. 177–190.

Klein, Melanie (1987). Frühstadien des Ödipuskonfliktes und der Über-Ich Bildung. In: *Die Psychoanalyse des Kindes*. Frankfurt am Main: Fischer.

Müller, Helena and Pomper, Desirée (2019). Sie sagten mir, dass ich heute eine richtige Frau werde. *20minuten.ch.*, 5 June 2019: pp. 2–3.

Pessoa, Fernando (2000). *29.11.1931*. Frankfurt am Main: Fischer.

Ramadan, Zana (2017). *Die verschleierte Gefahr: Die Macht der muslimischen Mütter und der Toleranzwahn der Deutschen.* Wien: Europa-Verlag.

Rivière, J. (1992). Aggression. In: Melanie Klein and Joan Rivière, *Seelische Urkonflikte. Liebe, Haß und Schuldgefühl.* Frankfurt am Main: Fischer: pp. 11–18.

Ruthven, Marlise (2010). *Der Islam.* Stuttgart: Reclam.

Saegesser, Barbara (2014). Psychoanalytische Arbeit mit BB's, Kleinkindern und Müttern in unterschiedlichen afrikanischen Ländern (Le travail psychanalytique avec les bébés, des petits enfants et des mères dans divers pays d'Afrique). *Schweizerische Gesellschaft für Psychoanalyse (SGPsa) Bulletin* No. 77 (Spring): 5–13.

Saegesser, Barbara (2015). Psychoanalytische Feldarbeit in Ostafrikanischen Städten I. In: Peter Bründl and Carl E. Scheidt (Eds.), *Spätadoleszenz: Identitätsprozesse und kultureller Wandel. Jahrbuch der Kinder- und Jugendlichen-Psychoanalyse*, vol. 4. Frankfurt am Main: Brandes und Apsel: pp. 211–238.

Saegesser, Barbara (2016a). Psychoanalytische Feldarbeit in ostafrikanischen Städten II. Elternschaft in ostafrikanischen Städten. In: Peter Bründl, Manfred Endres and Susanne Hauser (Eds.), *Elternschaft: klinische und entwicklungspsychologische Perspektiven. Jahrbuch der Kinder- und Jugendlichen-Psychoanalyse*, vol. 5. Frankfurt am Main: Brandes und Apsel: pp. 269–279.

Saegesser, Barbara (2016b). Un travail psychothérapeutique en marge de ma pratique psychoanalytique et de la culture islamique dans des villes d'Afrique de l'est. (Translation and adaptation of my original manuscript written in German.) Lausanne. *Tribune Psychanalytique* 13.

Saegesser, Barbara (2016c). Eine Skizze psychoanalytiquer Arbeit in ostafrikanischen islamischen Städten. Islamische religiös-weltliche Gesetze und Normen als Basis für Widerstand und Abwehrbewegungen von PatientInnen im Rahmen (situativ angepasster) psychoanalytischer Arbeit. (Zürich). *„A jour"*, 2.

Saegesser, Barbara (2017). Psychoanalytische Feldarbeit in ostafrikanischen Städten III. In: Peter Bründl and Fernanda Pedrina (Eds.), *Abklärung – Diagnose – Fallbeschreibung. Forschung und Behandlungsplan. Jahrbuch der Kinder und Jugendspezifischen-Psychoanalyse*, vol. 6. Frankfurt am Main: Brandes & Apsel: pp. 196–215.

Saegesser, Barbara (2018). Psychoanalytische Feldarbeit in ostafrikanischen Städten IV. Über Konzepte und Heilverfahren für psychosomatisch erkrankte Jugendliche im ostafrikanischen Umfeld. Theorie und Klinik. In: Peter Bründl and Carl E. Scheidt (Eds.), *Psychosomatische Prozesse. Ätiologie, Krankheitsverlauf und Behandlung. Jahrbuch der Kinder und Jugendspezifischen-Psychoanalyse*, vol. 7. Frankfurt am Main: Brandes & Apsel: pp. 198–217.

Schreiber, Constantin (2019). *Kinder der Koran.* Berlin: Econ.

9 The Quran, children's games and creative playing in the sands of El-Alamein

In privately organised orphanages, as soon as I enter, I can normally see whether visitors have been announced or around or not. The level of importance attached by the orphanages to visitors in connection with potential donations or possible political state intervention is easily identifiable to me, by the clothes the babies and kids wear for these occasions, and by the toys that suddenly materialise on the floor or in the children's small and old iron beds. The girls and the boys are dressed in some way sweeter and more showily than usual, for this occasion. In some orphanages, babies in their iron beds are in those moments almost buried in toys or have toys dangling above them. Often, visitors bring toys with them, especially in connection with various sponsorship schemes affordable also by the poor visitors, so that a great number of toys may be found piled up in one or another particular place or corner. On days with no visitors, the children's clothes are simple, and no toys appear either in the kids' beds or with the little ones playing on the floor. I have never made a comment or expressed a concern about all this at these orphanages – not wishing to touch a nerve.

To be at all able to take part in the everyday life of an orphanage, to be let alone to play, i.e. work with the children, I must think carefully about what to mention and what to leave unsaid. There are many issues which clearly harm the children but which I cannot address in too direct a way. I weigh up what I want to bring up.

I assess for myself the value to the children of all the toys that are available at the homes, how they might be seen by the care persons to disrupt the process and the fixed routine they have of "handling" the children. The children could get used to a particular toy, enjoy playing with it, also as a transitional object and then cry desperately if this important object is taken away. They can become jealous, which is, in any case, always fervently and passionately expressed. This happens, for example, when visitors come to make donations and step around and across the little ones, on the floor in their outdoor footwear, while the children fight each other for the tiniest morsel – it might be a speck of dirt – by hitting, scratching and biting each other in the process.

DOI: 10.4324/9781003451587-9

The Quran, children's games and creative playing in El-Alamein   79

But why this piling on of so many toys when important visitors are announced? Presumably, in certain orphanages, so these visitors can see how well looked after the children are, how well they are cared for, to which these piles of toys bear testimony. Maybe dolls, little animals and the like are seen as goods of luxury, intended for the individual child and, or so it would then appear, owned by that child. On my rare visits to private family homes in modest flats or similar, I have never come across many toys, except maybe for the odd ball. Seen in this light, the *concept of child and play* does exist, and, from a social viewpoint, the positive influence of play – and of toys – on a child's development is recognised. The visitors are to be impressed by what they see: we offer our children many toys to play with! Yet, this is all purely staged just for the visitors' benefit – and for the children it becomes reality for the very shortest of times only. The everyday situation for children at orphanages and in poor families regarding toys, and play, is very different.

I once put in empty small beds some small scraps of tissue for the children to suck and chew on, and to suckle – there are often no blankets in the cots on account of the heat and a shortness of funds – in the hope that the babies could fantasise and create personal transitional objects. This I did after I had tried to explain to the non-trained care persons the purpose and intention behind my planned action. The following day, all the scraps of material had vanished. I was told this was not appropriate, it was disturbing and might possibly be dangerous as these small bits might easily be swallowed.

What is the deeper reason for refusing the introduction of this small novelty? It appears that, in this rather conservative religious-political culture, even in the context of child development the introduction of something new is difficult to accept. It is seen as disruptive to the fixed, rigid regime of the "treatment" of the little ones; disturbing, because it might lead to deviations from the established so-called care plan.

Finally, there is the fact that I, as the stranger, a white woman, have attempted to introduce something new (which is reminiscent of former colonial times); a woman who has a different way anyway of touching these orphaned babies and who takes them somehow more seriously, interacts with them for longer, instead of simply ignoring them when, for example, they cry or scream. The jealousy among the often-changing care persons of the way in which I "dedicate" myself to the children is intense. The idea that I should be there to assist and support them, rather than spend my time with the small insiders of the orphanage, is probably the deeper reason behind this reaction.

There are two aspects to consider when deciding whether or not to accept the introduction of an innovation: Will it be something that is in accordance with the teachings of the Quran, and will it bring me relief and less work, or will it bring more? The care persons are generally members of the lowest social group. They are uneducated, mostly untrained women, who have almost never been to school. Girls, in general, tend to go to school for less

80 *The Quran, children's games and creative playing in El-Alamein*

long because attending school removes them from the mother's custody and control and, in an unfamiliar environment, their honour may be compromised. Without this maternal control, there is the danger of erotic or sexual seduction and the inevitable consequence is social ostracism. The Quran also states that men and women should educate themselves and accumulate knowledge and wisdom. The women working in these orphanages, however, seem mainly concerned about earning a small wage to try to make a living. The matter in hand, namely the welfare and care of the babies or small children in their charge, is not seldom of secondary importance to them. From this perspective, children at play, children with toys, children who are cheerful, enjoy romping around and are, at the same time, being humanely reared and understood, fail to fit into the concept of these auxiliary female persons, who are frequently exhausted already by the demands their own households place on them.

At one particular orphanage, during meal times for example, there existed between the boys (girls ate separately) and the care staff a kind of war game. The boys would dance about on the tables, then be forcefully sat down by, in some cases, physically fairly robust cooking and care women, whereupon they would be fed their meal by the female workers, spoonful by spoonful. All this was accompanied by almighty screaming and shouting: the children were screaming and the women, at the end of their tether, were loudly screaming back at them. After a while, I was able to introduce some peace and quiet into the proceedings in this small room. I explained to the care women that, given their ages of four to seven years, these kids were able to eat by themselves, and what eating a meal by themselves meant for children at that age. This, in turn, would bring relief to the care persons too. In this endeavour I actually succeeded, especially also because it resulted in the promised relief. The boys now ate by themselves, although they did lose the opportunity to combatively emerge either victorious or in defeat from their game.

Everything I have described so far occurred not in villages or small towns but in cities with, in some cases, millions of inhabitants.

In a domestic setting, in the care of the mother, a girl experiences considerably less freedom with regard to playing compared to boys. The mother engages the girl in cooking and housekeeping – she is, after all, to become an efficient housewife – which hardly leaves any opportunity for play. Boys, by contrast, carry out jobs outside the home, they move about more freely and are given more space also to play outside their home. For girls, household chores become substitutes for child's play. Here in East Africa, it is not play that is the main occupation of the child – as is mostly the case in Western European societies – it is *everyday chores that become the child's play*: for example, for boys who battle through on their own in huge street markets or in mazes of narrow alleys in places which, centuries ago, adopted labyrinthine layouts to foil pirate attacks. I can well imagine that this way of life must be dangerous, though at the same time thrilling in a playful

The Quran, children's games and creative playing in El-Alamein   81

way: to outwit others, to be smarter, more cunning than others and so on. Only, for many boys this is about real survival: surviving on the outside, or being imprisoned for acts of minor delinquency.

Yet, often it is household duties that become mostly a girl's play, such as minding siblings, caring for grandparents and single aunts, fetching water, cooking, washing (washing machines and vacuum cleaners are financially unattainable), sewing, cleaning, looking after a mother or a father, fishing, stealing and more.

In hospitals, along with a patient's mother and sisters, there are also many of the other children present where possible. All these people adapt to the patient's room, which is much too small. They sit and lie between the bedsteads (there are four to five patients in one room), they chat, they eat and poorer families do not normally carry toys with them. The quicker kids escape into the hospital corridors and run around – mostly the boys. The girls remain quietly and obediently sitting in the sick room. They may be given something to eat and drink. Children who are themselves sick in hospital are normally without toys as well, without a little animal toy or other such toys. To buy toys, too much money is needed.

Very simple play and psychotherapy with girls and boys

In one of these privately led orphanages (although apparently they were under state supervision), the management allocated children with difficult behaviour to me for therapy, at times warning me that these children were, for example, autistic, melancholic or wicked. Nevertheless, at least there was, with this psychologically slightly more aware directress, a concept of psychotherapeutic work with children in place.

Vignette 1: Boy E

His exact age is unknown. He was found at night behind a rubbish bin, almost fully dehydrated. He has possibly survived a past attempt at strangulation, since the skin on his neck shows strangulation marks, patches of hardened tissue and is entirely dried out. The police brought him to the home. He is referred to me as autistic. At first, I have hardly any idea where and how I am to move in this chaotic environment. I ask for a separate room for my therapeutic work. The rooms here are full of very loud noise caused by both children and adults, the latter incessantly telling the children off about something. Fortunately, in this particular orphanage, a room is found (the orphanage benefited from a rich donor) and they now offer to me – naturally I'm working in a humanitarian way – one empty room.

Of course, I assume that the boy can use the coloured pencils I have brought along to draw with. However, he has never seen coloured pencils. He uses them like Mikado sticks, like small bits of wood to play with. As soon as he understands that coloured pencils are really for colouring, he

82 *The Quran, children's games and creative playing in El-Alamein*

wants to use them to leave traces of colour everywhere – on walls, tables, bedsteads and so on. This later gets me into trouble with the management. E loves working physically, especially physically resisting something. He picks up something heavy and completely fails to concentrate on what he is doing. They are performance games which he invents for himself. For example, he lifts out the slatted frame from a wooden bed, then tries to pull out the slats from their frame underneath also and begins to use these materials to build a world of his own. He takes the slats to the window, to the mirror, to the table, creates new links. He also loves thrashing about with them – again due to his unconscious wish to build his own world. I partly feel threatened by these aggressive desires. A direct exchange with him is almost impossible: he cannot speak properly, also no Arabic, and our conversation happens with hands, gestures, looks and actions, ultimately also with the feet. I attempt to lead him out of his autistic skin, his shield of skin. I reiterate to him that I feel afraid when he lashes out with the wooden slats in my direction.

During my time with him, I always drink some tea that the directress gives me – out of a small mug or a flask. He observes me carefully, meticulously, imitates what I am doing with gestures. He has no mug. I buy him one, too. We now drink together at the same time. After some two or three psychotherapy sessions, he offers me his cup to drink from. From an initial distance between us, E develops a mutual, virtually mute contact full of expression (see his work with the wooden slats), then this extremely precise observation of my drinking, whereupon follows his imitation of this and finally, having fulfilled the desire for something life-sustaining, i.e. water (given that he was found practically dead from dehydration), the fervent wish to exchange something with me/with a human someone. He registers me as a living human being and becomes himself inwardly alive, sensitive and feeling. A living human being in contact with another. He has accepted me into his world as a person with whom to think, act and feel is possible. We get closer but at the same time I do not forget the simultaneous importance of maintaining psychotherapeutic distance.

When I return to East Africa for the third time within a year and enter the home, he comes walking towards me down a long corridor and fails to recognise me at first. Then, suddenly, there is this enormous scream, issuing from his innermost being and through him, like a sort of flash of lightning. It is his recognition of me that shakes him, and he runs towards me. This flash of recognition in a child who was two to three years old before being diagnosed as autistic, shows how closely together shock and exuberant joy lie within him.

Vignette 2: the daughter

A friend asks me whether I would speak to the daughter of one of his artist friends outside the hospital walls, outside the hospital's remit. The girl

The Quran, children's games and creative playing in El-Alamein 83

is a little confused, her father thinks she is "not normal". She is now in the process of finishing her school-leaving exams and it appears, so I am told, that she is highly intelligent. I agree to meet the young, adolescent woman. She wears attractive clothes: a synthetic shawl with a Scottish tartan print in beige, brown and black, cleverly imitating Western-European style and elegantly draped around her head. She has just passed an exam that is not easy. She lives with her father, an artist who, in his own words, is professionally successful and earns a comfortable salary. The parents are separated. The mother lives five hours away from her former husband. The girl desperately wishes to move in with her mother, away from her father and her current environment. In her new place, the mother has apparently set up a small stall for herself selling ladies' fashion. By talking to the father, I find access to his open-minded personality, and an agreement is found in keeping with the daughter's wishes. Later, I hear that she is doing well at her mother's.

In all my years of living and working in East Africa and in institutions of the countries there, I never heard a female patient say that she wanted to go and live with her father. However, they often wished to go and live with a progressively thinking aunt, for example. Different to girls in Western European societies, girls in East Africa seem to feel not comfortable enough with their fathers, not protected enough and without enough positive recognition. They are possibly so strongly influenced by local tradition that they believe, as a future wife, they need to learn housekeeping and motherhood from another woman.

Boys, by contrast, long for their fathers, who are often absent and happy to leave the task of bringing up his children, his sons, to their mother or grandmother. In psychotherapeutic work with small boys, the longing for the father always takes centre stage.

At the same time, sons principally tend to be terribly spoiled by their mothers. They are not asked to help in the household, and mothers try to make everything possible for their sons. As a result, many young men fail in life and develop a drug habit (especially when there are drug supply routes running nearby). In this respect, too, mothers who would never normally spend money on themselves manage to find money for their sons. The desire to spoil their sons and thus tie them to themselves is often greater than the capability to acknowledge the seriousness of the problem. I have worked on and off in a methadone programme in a small location and for this reason I am relatively familiar with the situation of young men and their financial dependence on their mothers.

All in all, the children's ways to play, and the types of play they engage in, are, I think, mostly also subject to Quranic norms. The play of children per se has almost no value or importance attached to it, especially not in the form of free play. A truly free, self-invented type of play, and the act of creative invention of either boys or girls, I practically never came across. Maybe the many prayers, five per day, also feature in a somehow interesting way as substitutes for a kind for play?

84 *The Quran, children's games and creative playing in El-Alamein*

Vignette 3: the freely chosen and creative play in El Alamein

I am in Egypt, walking alone through the desert sands of El Alamein, the site of terrible bloody battles in the Second World War. I am there long before tourism begins to take a hold in that area. Suddenly, I hit upon an array of torn and discarded cardboard boxes and polystyrene packaging, and oblong bits of shredded basketweave – what were originally probably very light crates used for the transport of poultry and other small animals. And inside these frame-like bits of debris, I find a tiny children's world, or, rather, an adult world, entirely crafted from selected items of more refuse such as bits and pieces of torn cloth, torn linoleum scraps, bits of carpet, rags and rubber car mats, drinking straws and lengths of wire, everything broken, tattered, threadbare and fraying at the edges. In this small, new world, there is a flower fashioned from a bit of old cloth; there is a torn piece of cardboard packaging which once held a beauty product, carrying a picture of a beautiful, dark-haired lady with black eyes and standing in its space almost like a sculpture; there is a photograph, the cover of a toilet cistern, old, torn shoes, old hair rollers. Evidently, in a place that was once a centre of war, a place where machines went up against machines, tanks against tanks, marked by death, horror and suffering all over. And now it's lying empty and desolate, just a small distance away from the mausoleum, the memorial of El Alamein. And here are now some children at play, or so I assume, creating from bits of rags and garbage a quiet, safe, protected world, a world in which there is a mother, a father, children. Fortunately, these children have discovered for themselves some sort of therapeutic work. A small miracle – the fact that this should have happened in a place once so full of utter carnage, where thousands of humans lost their lives; and here, out of a pile of discarded junk, new life has unfolded through the creativity of children.

I am thinking it might have been boys who created the frames and tore or cut the bits of carpets into shape; it might have been girls fashioning the dolls and interior furnishings – my Western European imagination at work. How it all happened in reality, given the current East African gender distribution in children's play, this time in the form of real play and not chores performed by children for or on behalf of adults that substitute for play, I cannot tell. I have only come across this "intact adult doll's-house-world" now that the children have accomplished it, put it together from bits and pieces most likely picked up in the sand and on the streets and, within the framework-providing materials, set it up; and then, within that world that they have built, they have brought to life the figures of various members of a family which they have fashioned for themselves.

I begin to take photographs. Also of the children, who slowly, slowly – only to quickly disappear again – begin to stick their heads out from behind the small sand dunes where they are hiding to watch me. I look back at them. Cautiously, hesitantly, they finally approach, one after the other, six

The Quran, children's games and creative playing in El-Alamein 85

boys and girls in all, to stand nearby, opposite me. They seem a little inhibited, yet at the same time curious enough about this white woman and her interest in the homes of their new created world. It quickly becomes clearer that I do not pose a danger to them, and vice versa. We talk together with our eyes, hands, fingers, ears and noses, and I photograph their work of art. This is what probably lures them from their hiding places completely in the end. They wish to be photographed – like most children in East Africa do and, of course, also often adults. I am not keen on taking photographs and rarely do so. For them, I now do so as a favour. For me personally, this widespread digital capturing of anything and everything we encounter goes against my deeper intentions; I find it too intrusive, especially so in foreign cultural places. What I notice in the East African environment (as I did also during my journey to Central Africa), however, is that severely depressed children's eyes and facial expressions hardly appear so anymore in the photographs. I take photos of them on their request – their eyes become shiny. East and Central African children are also fascinated by mirrors or reflecting glass and glass shards. They like seeing themselves in mirror images. One might think that this has to do with narcissistic personality traits and the concomitant desire to be truly noticed and fully apprehended. This symptom of their inner reality presumably grows out of a lack of lived and experienced narcissistic attention. I described this in more detail earlier in this book.

Their wish to be photographed – which to Western eyes seems mostly a tiny ask – this wanting to be noticed and apprehended by means of a supposedly expensive piece of equipment, this (especially by small children) narcissistically highly valued way of being noticed and preserved, seems for a short time to evoke strong feelings of self-fulfilment or self-elevation. Having been photographed and preserved in a picture, the children can look at and study themselves at leisure. And in these photos the depressed facial expressions in the children's faces and eyes seem to have been blown away and hidden beneath what appear to be sunny, beaming smiles.

Vignette 4: the shy, sensitive, distanced boy

I try to interest the little ones in a game where we sit in a circle. A small boy keeps away. He stands to one side, and I leave him be, just the way he seems to want it. I try to play very simple games, games which, in essence, are only the beginning of play. For example, standing in a small circle and then sitting down. The little boy stays outside the circle, the way he normally remains a little at a distance, and from this safe distance he observes what happens. He is sweet-looking, appears alert, perky and curious but, at the same time, extremely cautious and shy vis-à-vis others. I leave him in his place, a place he has chosen for himself where he probably feels safe enough, and I concentrate on those children who are happy to participate. I keep my hands behind my back. Suddenly, I feel something touching

86   *The Quran, children's games and creative playing in El-Alamein*

one of my hands, light as a feather, and for a fraction of a second only. I look behind me and there he is: the little boy in his lop-sided pyjamas who always stands to one side, looking up at me and, at the same time, with his tiny fingers, almost not touching my own. He is very shy and at the same time finds his own way to begin to work with all the others. He has searched for and found me in his own way. His whisper-like signal of contact touches me deeply.

Vignette 5: swimming (almost) girls in the sea

At times, I see how young girls try to swim – I see this equally as a form of play of the body with water. Sometimes, when in the sea, I am asked by young girls whether I would teach them to swim. These obviously seem to be very freely brought up girls, as they are splashing about in the sea wearing "normal" swimsuits and not the all-veiling types prescribed by their religion, and they seem to be allowed to go into the sea – or are doing so anyway. I normally explain, with hands and feet, as we have no common language and I speak their version of Swahili only sparingly, how it works and encourage them not to give up immediately.

Vignette 6: working with young people in a Catholic aid organisation

The organisation prioritises the Catholic faith and holds and pursues – in a part of the world entirely dominated by Muslim religion, culture and politics – missionary intentions. I see the young people in their charge play and fool around outside the small mission house, "speak" with them and later attempt to work with this organisation, i.e. with these children. The organisation supports somehow – for Catholic religious reasons – the demeaning and destructive East African Muslim attitude towards girls. The organisation looks after street children, boys as well as girls. It offers them meals (not daily) and access to running water in a small courtyard, so they can wash themselves as well as their own clothes and possibly blankets, and dry them on a washing line made available for the purpose. There is room to play and climb trees, and some sort of advisory service. The organisation is situated in a relatively small, but politically important town. These parent-less, neglected children are not allowed to spend the night in the rooms of this Catholic mission but are made to clear out of the small courtyard and garden into the street. They sleep crouched under buildings, under market stalls, outside the city in the sand or, if they can gain access, in the harbour. I offer the organisation my humanitarian collaboration, as I see a lot of despair and a certain amount of hope in the eyes of the children when I approach them on the small road leading to the small mission house. Yes, one is, after internal consultation and with some reluctance, prepared to work with me. I am not being fully

The Quran, children's games and creative playing in El-Alamein   87

trusted, and they say: "You can only work with the street children if you promise not to talk to the girls about sexual matters, and especially not about contraception." The boys are not mentioned. I agree, but from my point of view it is exactly this issue that is of pressing urgency. The street girls are mostly children of single or raped mothers. If these girls are not being protected against rape, by answering their questions about sex and by a small amount of sexual education, the danger of this happening to them, considering the inhabitants of the neighbourhoods in which the girls roam, and given the girls are adolescent or not yet even this age, is extremely high. The town is full of soldiers stationed there as well as other men, which considerably increases the danger of street children, both boys and girls, being attacked and raped. The children, above all girls, come to me and are most excited about being able to talk to me – I am wearing jeans like them and not a religious habit. From the start, they talk to me in English, a language I know – they learn it on the street – and they are desperate to learn and know about sexual "things". At the same time, they feel embarrassed, but not embarrassed enough as they real-ise the urgency of being able to exchange with someone on the matter. I ask them, amongst other things, why they are living on the streets and whether they have no homes to go to. I talk in the direction of, but not directly about, contraception and serious, potentially fatal illnesses with which they could be infected.

The organisation in question does not really safeguard these children against any of the dangers mentioned, although it proclaims on a worldwide basis that it is an organisation that offers shelter and protection. After three and a half working days and great acceptance amongst the young street girls, I am no longer granted access to the mission. I insist to be informed about the reason for this decision. I am told I have broken the taboo on speaking about sexual issues, about contraception. My arguments for how vitally important for life and survival such information is for these girls are brushed aside. The taboo is based and defended on the principles of the Catholicism underlying this organisation. There is to be no contraception, even if, by maintaining this attitude, the tradition of young, unmarried girls being raped and impreg-nated and, under Quranic doctrine, then socially ostracised, is continued with these female Catholic carers' full awareness. These carers allow these girls to descend into the same personal and social misery and despair as their mothers did. Catholicism here contributes to the ruin of girls and plays into the hands of Quranic law. Under Islam, the main religion of the region, unmarried mothers are, as already indicated, socially marginalised and cast out. What is for the feminine a wholly negatively tinged gender differentia-tion is, concerning female sexuality, exercised and defended by Catholicism hand in hand with Islam.

I would very much have liked to talk to the boys as well, but the time admitted to me was too short to allow any chance of that.

88 *The Quran, children's games and creative playing in El-Alamein*

There are international organisations such as Save the Children, Médecins sans Frontières, SOS Kinderdorf and many others, with whom I interacted on an intermittent basis as long as they were interested in my ideas, my concepts and my work. With these organisations, children at play are something natural, and boys and girls are, as far as I can see, treated as equals. I saw children play in the gardens of these institutions or, at times, sit outdoors in little groups eating nuts, and no evident difference seemed to be made between girls and boys, not in the furniture inside the accommodation and not in the types of game the children played. In Quran-oriented areas, girls are not normally seen playing outside – they are requested to help in the house and household. The work of all these organisations is being allowed to continue despite the fact that they do not observe the gender differentiation imposed by Quranic law.

I have so far not had the opportunity to speak to someone who has also worked with children in East Africa to exchange experiences. I know, above all, my own East African experiences of short therapies with small children that I have initiated on my own accord. In East African regions, such therapies are unfamiliar. Children who rebel are passed on. Within families, girls are forced to work in the house and to be of help wherever needed. Boys, by contrast, are nurtured, may perhaps get hold of a bicycle one day, and they are also the ones who tend to develop a drug habit.

It is questionable whether child's play, the European concept of child's play, can ever be considered in this region. For adults, play is part of life. Men repeatedly engage in play. They regularly congregate in restaurants or rooms to play their games. Women possibly do not, I cannot tell. Children – so it seems to me – mostly do not.

10 Concepts and treatments for psychosomatic patients in the East African environment

> Should one tell everything? Should one make a choice? Should one embellish the events? I think one needs to tell everything.
>
> (Leiris, Michel. Diary entry, 28 December 1931. Reproduced in Leiris (1985), Part One, Diary, p. 19)

In the following thoughts and descriptions, and always in my field research reports from East Africa, I refer to my earlier field research reports (Saegesser 2017)[1] and to everything I have seen, found, heard, participated in, witnessed and considered in various cultures and ethnicities, in institutions, in familial contexts and in other special groups.

I usually enter or study the discussed new research environment with little specific prior theoretical knowledge. For the past 14 years, I have been observing, learning about and trying to understand better the possible cultural, political-religious, ethno-psychoanalytical and complex human connections and combinations. I have been learning directly as well as indirectly from the actions and behaviour of pregnant women, mothers, sisters, aunts, midwives, women doctors, carers, and at times also husbands, from conversations with them, and from conversations with colleagues who are professionally active in orphanages, hospitals and in psychiatry.

Psychosomatic thinking and working in medical institutions and groups

I have worked as a psychoanalyst in several medical institutions in East Africa. As far as I can see, and compared to corresponding Western European theories and knowledge, the term psychosomatic and certain basic psychosomatic models are practically unknown here. In the hospital, I try to address this and try to explain the basic Western European concept of this illness – demonstrating directly, where possible, on actual hospitalised patients with psychosomatic illness, for example an anorexic girl. My audience tends to listen, shows interest, but remains, above all, wary. "How does it come about that so much potency, dynamism and power

DOI: 10.4324/9781003451587-10

90 *Concepts and treatments for psychosomatic patients in East Africa*

are attributed to the psyche?" is probably their question. Younger hospital doctors appear extremely overstretched. They are too few in number, often not fully qualified, extremely badly paid, and yet active and working with almost no supervision. They hasten along mostly dark hospital corridors and feel stressed and unsupported. One of their most frequent reactions and attitudes seems to indicate: nothing new, please! Maybe also: please, nothing new, complicated or time-consuming from a white woman, a "near-colonial". In theory, this new model of illness and the corresponding medical treatment may be of interest, but putting it into practice appears, for several reasons, impossible. Also, as I see it, there is a lack of psychiatric-psychological support, above all on account of the fact that psychology remains an unfamiliar field.

The more experienced and successful amongst the doctors believe they do not require new concepts in their work. They feel they have been doing well enough so far with their existing knowledge. There is neither the requirement nor the custom to engage in further training. Conditions in East African institutions are in many respects not comparable with institutions in probably Western Africa and certainly Western Europe.

The psychological dimension

It is possible that some medical doctors have read about psychosomatic issues. But the psychological dimension plays an imperative role in it. And this psychological dimension, in their eyes, should play no part in the definition of the somatic and, speaking generally, not play a part at all in anything. This is in complete contrast to a big part of Western European thinking and understanding.

The role that individual-subjective psychological processes play in humans, and in the understanding of humans, is barely recognised. Consequently, the same applies to psychology, and even more so to psychotherapy and psychoanalysis. The psychological dimension and the psychological process and its specific dynamics are described but not as psychological ones, rather as human possibilities to act, given by Allah and in this sense covered and claimed in the Quran. Somatic trends are in this view "real facts" and all conditions of human existence seem to be facts. Human emotions are as written in the Quran and, insofar as they are "allowed" and tolerated, clearly designed and described. This structuring may, for example, take the form of the hypostasised effect of evil and other spirits. In the words of the philosopher Immanuel Kant, substantial reality is insinuated and attributed to the idea of the existence of ghosts or spirits. As such, the psychic is not per se something very important and subjective, but something that manifests openly or covertly in emotions and symptoms of illness. These symptoms enter the human being in the form of and through spirits from the outside, a non-human entity, something God-given and this way made substantial by divine decree. In East

Africa, these spirits are called Djins. For many East African people, the idea that the psychic carries a certain subjectivity and performs some sort of determining power over the physical would appear eerie and somehow not possible. The physical, by contrast, is representative of what is familiar, what is accepted, not least because it is "graspable". For Western Europeans on the other hand, the idea of their psychic processes being triggered and influenced by alien or evil spirits that have entered their bodies unnoticed would appear eerie and somehow impossible. Here I do, of course, clearly exclude the symptomatology of certain Western European mental disorders.

Psychological processes and the Quran

The mental, individual and subjective side of a subject falls, in a life environment entirely subsumed by the Quran and by Quranic law and doctrine, completely away. It simply does not exist as there is only Allah as well as Allah's devout believers. My psychoanalytical interpretation is: humans cannot subjectify themselves but are and must remain a self-object of Allah. Humans are creations of Allah, and it is Allah who considers, decides and directs them.

In the psychiatric department and rooms where I have worked, psychiatric symptoms and their cures are often known because of the *medication used*. Psychotherapeutic work, however, especially with psychosomatic patients, is carried out to a very limited extent only, if at all. Advances in the recognition of psychosomatic symptomatology are occasionally made in the treatment of severely heroin- or cocaine-addicted patients.

The significance of medical doctors, helping persons and healers in psychosomatic care

Psychotropic drugs are mainly the responsibility of, and frequently prescribed by, a (psychiatric) doctor; afterwards they are distributed to the patients by the helping female persons or even by self-service – at times they are "offered" from quite large open boxes in a fairly risky way.

What I have noticed, and what is discussed with me openly, are the many healing cures that are not approved in Western Europe. These cures are provided by healers who, depending on the region, culture and language, are called by different names. A frequent name is Manga. Djins, as already mentioned, are evil spirits (occasionally also good ones), which carry out their evil deeds inside the body – from the head of the human being down. This acting is difficult to understand, especially in Western European thinking, where they take on sinister dimensions. The various courses of treatment offered by healers represent small, serious businesses in which many East African people place a deep trust rooted in old tradition. I think that especially in this context psychosomatic symptoms are

92 *Concepts and treatments for psychosomatic patients in East Africa*

being taken seriously to a certain extent. This seems to be a result of an enormous amount of specific knowledge and ability, handed down orally through the generations, which does bring about relief and cure.

The WHO as well as the African Union (AU) have published reports on Traditional African Medicine (TAM) and listed all of the illnesses for which TAM practitioners promise a cure; in some instances these are extremely severe, such as AIDS and cancer. There appear to be no records of the healing practices and processes involved, mainly because healers cannot write and, possibly, prefer not to keep written records of their practices. Traditional knowledge and practice are almost always passed on orally. In this way, none of the knowledge performed can be copied or plagiarised.

I have had the chance to speak with two healers (see below). The leader of psychiatry took me to see them, as he himself took a great interest in the work of healers. He wanted to conduct a study on the subject and was awaiting a research grant. He was working together with selected Mangas – they referred patients to him or vice versa. This worked on the basis of his own and the healers' common Muslim faith and acceptance of the concept of Djins, the (often) evil spirits working in the human body and bringing about the illnesses to be treated. Djins are named variously in different cultures. This collaboration by the head of the local psychiatric service is not necessarily usual, but from a healing principle and healing process angle sensible and quite necessary. According to the WHO, 80% of people, specifically in the eastern Sub-Saharan region, consult healers, not least because of a shortage of medically trained persons. In the past, many colonial rulers banned healers and natural healing, possibly on account of the fact that they found these processes suspicious and uncontrollable. To some extent there might also have been an element of superstitious fear that they themselves and their families might be put under some evil spell.

Michel Leiris' contribution

As far as I am aware, Michel Leiris (1985, p. 8) was one of the first to report in a frank and unembellished manner on the various cults and healing ceremonies which he came across during his travels through the African continent. He joined a French delegation, headed by his friend Marcel Griaule, which embarked on a trip to Africa. From 1931 to 1933, the group conducted ethnological research from west to east, from Dakar to Djibouti. In his "Phantom Africa" diary, he describes extensively the cultural, magical, long-winded mask ceremonies of the Dogon (Mali) and the magic Zar possession cults found in many parts of Ethiopia (Abyssinia in those days). Heinrichs wrote in his foreword: "'Phantom Africa' is both a masterpiece and a document . . ., testimony of an attempt to live and to survive, to overcome boredom, and to capture the magical . . . 'Phantom

Concepts and treatments for psychosomatic patients in East Africa 93

Africa' documents the colonial origins of ethnology and what individual researchers have made from it" (Leiris 1985, p. 8). Leiris' descriptions are especially interesting because he does not gloss over the reality he witnesses. He observes all actions with serious attention, in exact detail, conscientiously and with great care; he describes all this, as he himself states, "as the secretary, archivist, examining magistrate, supervisor and bureaucrat accompanying them". Unusually for his time, he also reports on his own psychic reactions, his feelings of counter-transference, unaware of the existence of such a term to describe the various mental conditions he was experiencing. His inner attitude and his writing correspond already in 1931 to the ethno-psychoanalytic method, in which especially the intersubjective effect gains in importance. Leiris at the same time distances himself from those then current methods and auxiliary constructions of certain ethnologists, for example Malinowski, who postulated the model of participatory observation, possibly as a strategy to not become inwardly involved in the ongoing processes. One must distance oneself, with a positivistic attitude, in order not to be drawn in too much and touched too much. Leiris described ethnology as fundamentally colonialist: one often robs the peoples and ethnic communities of Africa of their most holy possessions, those possessions which are vital for the performance of healing rituals by healers, as those are mostly statues and objects containing empowering qualities. One does so in order to exhibit them in museums at home.[2] "All ethnologists know this," Leiris wrote, "but nobody writes about it" (1985, p. 6). Except: Leiris did. This did not make him popular with everyone.

Given the considerable level of authenticity in his diary, this should present an opportunity to pinpoint conflicts among people of different cultures and to describe communication and interaction problems. The state of science, writes Leiris (1985, Part I, p. 6), becomes more recognisable at the level of conflictual experience than at the level of knowledge and ideals.

> Such conflicts arise between white and indigenous people, the latter being robbed and exploited by the former over and over again. And, finally, certain groups of indigenous people, for example the Abyssinians and the Dogons, collaborate with the French ethnologists and play into the hands of the white people; they take to them and sell them their most holy objects and, along with these, also an important, integral part of themselves.
>
> (Leiris 1985, Part One, Foreword)

Leiris finally admits to the fact that he himself treated the "savages" no better than did his colleagues (1985, p. 8).[3]

For ethnology, it would probably be more comfortable if this diary had never been written, or if it were to enjoy less prominence than it does.

94   *Concepts and treatments for psychosomatic patients in East Africa*

Heinrichs states bluntly: "The ethnologist, as described by Leiris, is in many respects no better than the most hard-working industrialist who robs the labourer of his last penny: the ethnologist robs the 'savages' of everything. With the objects they have stolen, they have kidnapped 'their life'" (Leiris 1985, Part I, Foreword, p. 8). Leiris himself writes: "I am still feeling dejected. Sometimes I feel like smashing everything to bits. . . . Slowly but surely, they all go along with the pious lie and make their peace with Heaven" (1985, Part I, p. 168).

Hospital or healer

Many patients are suspicious of hospitals. Before their hospital stay, they would often already have seen a healer, or they intend to see one if they feel that the medical doctors at the hospital will not help them, or that an evil spirit, a Djin, is making them or their family ill.

In my "Western" thinking, I had assumed that predominantly physical complaints such as a broken leg, or bone fractures in general – physical pain impairing physical well-being – would increase the chance of a hospital referral, because the life of the injured person might be in danger. I thought that in such situations a hospital referral was mandatory, especially also because the injury is physical, obvious to the naked eye and cannot be concealed. The WHO, however, states things differently: priority is given to healers.

In my work on parenthood (Chapter 4), I consider issues of shame in the East African environment. I mention, amongst other things, attempts by the extended family to conceal difficulties from the outside world. Such difficulties would include personal health issues and health problems of the children. One explanation for this might be the idea that sick children bear testimony to bad parenting. It would be interesting to investigate in more detail whether society attaches a similar stigma to parents whose sick child is seen as being possessed by an evil spirit or whether, in similar cases, the parents are not implicated. I have, so far, not been able to pursue this question further and in any case, my initial unbiased hypothesis – later statistically falsified – was that minor or chronic complaints would be more likely to be presented to a healer. Chronic complaints are by their nature not immediately visible to neighbours, and in hospitals – in most respects very different to Central European hospitals – they are not likely to be recognised as psychosomatic illnesses. And chronic illnesses, like many other complaints, are not publicly talked about.

My first hypothesis was the following: for psychosomatic complaints, which are not regarded as such but seen as caused by evil spirits (a Djin or a Zar), and a person being possessed by such a spirit, it is primarily a healer who is consulted, or various healers. If complaints persist, medical treatments are chosen either exclusively, or parallel to those of healers. Should medical treatments fail, further healers are sought.

Concepts and treatments for psychosomatic patients in East Africa   95

My initial perception, that consulting a healer was something that needed to be concealed from others, I now realise was wholly based on Western thinking and corresponds not at all to East African reality. It is possible that it is the exact opposite which is true: opting for hospital treatment instead of traditional healing methods is something to be embarrassed about. In the East African environment, hospitals often suffer from an extremely bad reputation. I was warned about the hospital, at which I later began to work, in the following terms: "Be careful; should you fall ill, never go to this hospital. The only way you'll leave it, is as a dead person."

Visiting two healers

And now I present two encounters I had with two famous, much-consulted healers, arranged by and together with the director of the psychiatric department of a medical hospital. The director was a highly intelligent, mentally astute person, flexible and agile in his dealings, widely travelled, and completed his medical degree in a, for him, foreign language and foreign cultural environment with a different political ideology and (mostly Christian) religion. He once said to me excitedly: "You know, there is, for example, a truly famous healer who, unfortunately, lives miles away from here on a small island. He's about 100 years old. He is familiar with about 100 spirits, can accurately differentiate between them and diagnose their effects with great precision."

The first Manga, dressed in jeans and a shirt with an appliquéd "Crocodile", meets us in his herbal shop in the middle of the village. Herbal healers are common in Sub-Saharan regions and are part of a centuries-old, or maybe millennia-old, tradition. To begin with, we speak English. He talks about his herbal cures and about the countless different herbs he uses, possibly 100, possibly 200, maybe 1,000 – I cannot tell. Then, I would like to learn about his diagnostic process. Initially, I tell him in basic terms how I proceed in my own Western European practice. Then I would also like to know about his own concepts. But to my question of how he distinguishes between psychotic and neurotic symptoms, when I describe to him different symptomatic features, he has no answer to give. He explains that in each individual patient's case he forms a specific picture and then decides on a course of treatment. It may be that he sees a patient twice a week, or just once, or once a month, or once every two months, and so on. I think this may also lead to transference and healing through transference. Finally, after a longish conversation, I ask him whether he could perhaps let his patients write or draw. I tell him I am interested to see how he makes his diagnosis, or how I might, with the help of my graphological knowledge and my extensive work with East African patient drawings, be able to understand and explain for myself his way of establishing a diagnosis. I tell him that in this way I shall probably be able to form a clearer picture of

96 *Concepts and treatments for psychosomatic patients in East Africa*

how he has, based on his decades-long experience, been able to accumulate his knowledge and how he keeps supplementing it. He replies that this might be difficult. The people coming to him for help would not write or draw "just like that". However, when I come again, we can come back to it. He says he is interested in speaking with me and he would invite me to his home so that we can spend the entire day in discussion. This time round, I am not able to accept his offer.

The other Manga we visit lives in a remote place. The track leading to his home has been hollowed out by tropical storms and is hard to find. Finally, we manage to get there. It becomes clear already from the outside that this is probably a place for ceremonial rituals. The healing compound is a kind of small bungalow with at least three rooms. One room has a wrought-iron gate which can be closed and such gates are uncommon in deprived surroundings. The Manga, dressed in a black kaftan, awaits in front of the house to greet us and we enter together. The healer seems wary – attentive, and yet with a strict expression on his face and making some stiff gestural movements. It may be that he feels uncomfortable talking to a woman who is not there as his patient. At the same time, however, it is perceived as an honour for European interest to be shown in his work. As we enter, we cross a room in which two women are seated, surrounded by two or three men. We enter a tiny consultation room, where we try, in a mixture of English and Swahili (the director of the hospital translates for me), to have a conversation. Here, the exchange is not as relaxed, informative and differentiated as with the previous healer. There are about five assistants sitting in on the conversation. They hardly speak. From a physical stature point of view, they are totally different from their teacher: they are of a muscular, stocky build and young and their facial expressions are dull – save for one who appears livelier and more interested. These assistants seem to me fairly clumsy or, in the case of one of them, unexpectedly fanatical. They strike me as not very sensitive. The healer himself, also the manager of the establishment, comes across as being much given to the ceremonial; he looks ascetic-spiritual and, at the same time, very rational. After our unfortunately not very fruitful talk, he allows me to observe what is about to happen in the larger room – assistants proceeding with the exorcism of Djins, or ghosts.

The exorcism of Djins – acts of healing

Two girls are sitting on the floor, with one man sitting close by one of the girls, facing towards her ear. Working from the heel of his hand, he inserts an extremely long, pointed index finger underneath the girl's headscarf, where he rests it on her centre parting.

Twisting his finger from side to side, it is as if he were boring into her head (see Figure 10.1).

Concepts and treatments for psychosomatic patients in East Africa 97

Figure 10.1 A finger twisting from side to side, as if boring into the head.
Barbara Saegesser

At the same time, he shouts and sometimes screams suras for exorcisms into the girl's ear. His voice becomes steadily louder and is quite rhythmic and in addition, with his strong, weirdly overstretched and still twisting index finger he repeatedly knocks the girl on the head, as if he were trying to funnel the suras simultaneously into her head and into her ear. The knocking with the index finger becomes harder and harder. The chant of the suras swells to a hammer-like intensity. Then the excitement subsides, only to be taken up anew by further boring of the index finger, gradually increasing again in both intensity and pressure. During this performance, this student and Manga's assistant works himself, inwardly as I see it, into a state of arousal, a trance, so to speak, or sexual arousal. All this finds expression in his urging, pushing, self-exciting sequence of bodily movements and in certain particular-sounding noises that he utters. Half an hour later, although I am not exactly certain of how much time has passed, the girl emits a short, high scream, and the assistant healer ends his exorcism. Evidently a Djin, or one of the Djins, did leave the body of the treated girl.

98 Concepts and treatments for psychosomatic patients in East Africa

I feel very afraid, trapped. I feel I am not getting enough air; I want to run from the house – and yet I am inwardly deeply shocked, furious also, and worried about the welfare of the girl. During the ceremony, I would like to shout out and scream: "Stop torturing this woman right now!" As soon as the director of the psychiatric department notices my discomfort, he whispers: "It's all about chasing the spirits away. One has to frighten them, scare them, so that they flee from the body." Is this about evil spirits, or is this about the chastisement and subjugation of women?

In the next room, the one that is closed by a wrought-iron gate, a young woman lies on the floor. Except for what I am about to see, I unfortunately learn nothing further about her, and I will not meet her again later. I feel quite confused, fearful and threatened without actually having been physically assaulted. I can therefore only superficially report and analyse what I witness next. The woman appears to me to be vigorously fighting three men who are busying themselves with her on the floor. The ritual is similar to that with the girl. Suras are being shouted, or screamed rather, into her ear and bored into her head. The fact that the woman is actively struggling against all this is being interpreted to mean that the Djins are resisting the exorcism – they refuse to leave the body. As a result, the woman is being forcibly grabbed and held down by the legs and the arms. This is in addition to the treatment she is being subjected to on her head and in her ears. Then, of course, there is the wrought-iron gate, which remains firmly shut. The specially selected suras continue to be screamed into her ear. Giving a clearer description is, as already indicated, difficult for me, as I feel myself affected by my observations and by my counter-transference-like witnessing of the first Djin exorcism (see Figure 10.2).

Later on, the healer, the hospital director and I retire to the small consulting room. The two girls, whose healing I first observed and who were treated individually by one healing assistant or healing student only, join us there. The girls seat themselves next to me. They smell strongly of sweat, cold sweat, and remain silent – or have been silenced – and they seem exhausted. I ask the older girl how she feels. She says she feels tired but that her headache has gone. I ask why she doesn't take medicine to treat her headache. She doesn't like that, she replies.

I asked myself (Saegesser 2017) whether being possessed by evil spirits and the exorcisms earn the girl greater narcissistic weight within her family than medicine would. Being possessed affects the family environment harder, and the possessed girl may receive more recognition than she normally would, if she receives any at all. Surely, for these girls and women it is important for their survival to become narcissistically positively accepted and recognised, even if this way of recognition via the exorcism appears to be – in Western European thinking and perception – extremely painful, degrading, dangerous, denigrating and damaging; psychoanalytically seen, it seems to be a sadomasochistic treatment. I work on the assumption that a girl who, within her family, receives little respect on account of the

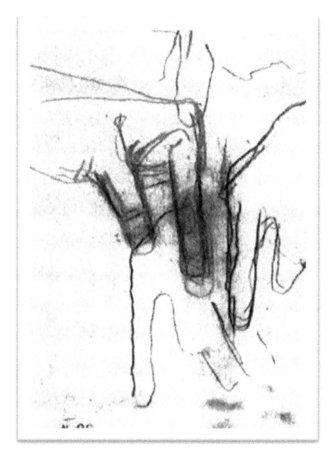

Figure 10.2 Sketch of a counter-transference. Pushing and threatening index fingers, simultaneously being confusingly overstretched and dancing with sadistic lust.

Barbara Saegesser

fact that she is "only" a girl (as is true for all women in Eastern Africa) will gain more attraction as a patient if she is obsessed by evil spirits than if she suffers her illness in silence and quietly eats her medicine.

It is possible, however, that my hypothetically developed, psychoanalytical Western thinking does not apply here.

Vignettes

Anorexic girl patient in the hospital room

My next vignette is on one of the anorexic girl patients who lies in the large room at the hospital. She is visibly anorexic. Another anorexic girl lying in

100 *Concepts and treatments for psychosomatic patients in East Africa*

the same room, but whose psychosomatic illness I will talk through in a completely different way, I present as a vignette in Chapter 11.

This anorexic very ill girl exists, as I see it, in a mutually fiercely clinging, symbiotic relationship with her mother. The care persons in the hospital room fail to understand what is wrong with the girl. The little girl's illness has a different background compared to the patient I shall describe in Chapter 11. I try to explain to the auxiliary person how I understand her illness. One of the medical doctors expresses an interest, listens, asks questions, wants to follow my instructions. He decides finally on a course of treatment of which he expects quicker results: blood transfusion, artificial feeding and folic acid. The girl refuses to let go of her mother, and I never have exclusive access to her. The mother acts like a loyal servant to her anorexic girl and vis-à-vis me behaves in a perfectly correct, but very reticent manner.

On the second day, when I try to make the mother leave for a moment to allow me to talk to the little patient alone, a northern European, fully qualified, nurse jumps in and explains firmly to me that the little girl needs her mother. She seems to assume that I know as little about the reasons of the girl's illness as she does.

Finally, the little girl is being fed artificially. She loses increasingly more weight and, without anyone asking for my opinion, is discharged from hospital. One morning, as I enter the room, she has simply vanished.

From a European diagnostic viewpoint, I would have thought that the symbiotic relationship between mother and child was maintained so that the mother would find a sense in life and a life-preserving reason to exist. As is often the case, I have no background information here and I am also left in the dark about the beginning of the girl's psychosomatic illness. There was no chance of talking alone with either the patient or the mother (for help with translation I would have been able to rely on helping members, at times medical doctors, hospital workers, cleaners, etc.). Both mother and child adopted a defensive attitude towards me. Reasons for unconscious motives for this possibly fatal symbiotic psychosomatic behaviour can be found in culturally and religiously firmly fixed social structures. Is it possible that the husband has introduced a second or a third wife into the family? This triggers serious psychic narcissistic crises and anxieties of loss in many women, which outwardly they do not show and about which they do not speak. Such a psychic crisis of the mother may have been the cause of this mutual clinging to each other and the grave illness of the daughter. The husband's behaviour of taking up to four wives accords with Quranic teachings about what is God's will. In other words – I add with some bitterness – one such teaching says this will not hurt the current wife who now has competition under her own roof for twenty-four hours a day. And another says: a new wife to the husband is not supposed to negatively affect the wife who is already there.[4]

Concepts and treatments for psychosomatic patients in East Africa   101

The little orphaned baby boy in withdrawal from khat

How strongly psychosomatic problems determine the path of life, and not seldom the path to death, especially also in the tiniest of human beings and babies, I have witnessed often in orphanages (Saegesser 2014, 2015).

My next vignette is of a tiny male baby, a roughly four-month-old and I diagnose him as, amongst other things, a baby with withdrawal symptoms. V is an orphan, or he was given away as if he were an orphan, and in this geographical region, especially men, but increasingly also women, chew khat (*catha edulis*). Khat is a naturally growing evergreen plant, resembling tall, bushy grass. Its effects are like that of amphetamines (it contains cathin). It buoys the mood but also triggers aggression and phantasms of grandeur. The plant is chewed, like tobacco used to be in Western Europe. A side-effect of chewing khat is diabetes, which has now become the number one disease of East Africa. Khat, the "nature drug", dehydrates the body, and in order to quench the resulting thirst, sugary drinks are used. In some African nations, khat is the national drug, daily imported by the state from neighbouring countries and, from 12 noon onwards, put on sale from small stalls along main roads. The takings, amounting to millions of dollars, all go to the state – this in countries where many die from starvation. At state banquets, or so I am told, khat is served on silver platters for the dignitaries and the president to enjoy (although I have never personally witnessed this).

Little V is on the brink of giving up. It appears that the world has given up on him, and he has been placed in the darkest, stony little side-room available at the orphanage. As medicine, and for his healing, a few crumbs of incense have been lit. Incense is often used especially in houses for orphans, as it is extremely cheap, acts as a disinfectant and is said to be particularly effective against colds. V suffers from severe bronchitis. He breathes heavily and presents with a swollen, cramped and distorted little face – probably mostly on account of his withdrawal symptoms. He no longer makes contact, and it is impossible to tell at first whether he will be interested in his life or succumb to his overpowering illnesses. With my attention and some slightly transformed psychoanalytic work[5] (as always in my East African work, based on my inner psychoanalytic frame), he begins to acknowledge me, to look at me, to become calmer and more relaxed, to hum along with me and to smile a little, to become steadily livelier. His facial expression changes, as does the colour of his little face, from yellow to light brown. We play for a bit with our hands, we hum and we smile. I massage his tiny feet,[6] and it becomes clear that he is on the way to getting better and healing.

As I come back, after three months' work in my own practice in Europe, I cannot find little V anywhere. I ask about him. "Oh," they reply, "we don't know him." However, I know for a fact that almost all of them do know

102 *Concepts and treatments for psychosomatic patients in East Africa*

him. I am then taken by a local medical colleague to administration. I am told little V has been given away for adoption, to the USA, and that there is no longer any documentation available.

I rebel inwardly, I despair and I say to my local colleague: "This cannot be true. No children from here are sent to the USA, and certainly not within the space of three months. Little V has died." He died – so I am told later – shortly after I had left.

I believe little V would have been able to continue to improve, had I not had to return to Europe. There should have been someone taking an interest in him, being interested in learning something from me and continuing my work with the little boy. But the care persons at that orphanage consist of auxiliary aides, extremely poor women, sometimes themselves former orphans from the same orphanage. They come from the lowest social classes and are paid a pittance. The rooms in such orphanages would be unimaginable in Western European conditions. In some cases, the orphaned babies are laid or "stuffed" into windowless, basement-like stony rooms. In East African orphanages, collaboration with their mostly untrained staff is generally very difficult. I upset established practice if I suggest and demonstrate alternative ways of working that would be more beneficial for the little children. What I want to introduce would cause the staff more work and require more personal commitment. Many of them seem very depressed and despondent. Learning something new and then applying it in practice seems an impossible challenge to meet. An added difficulty is probably also the fact that I am white and foreign. I am someone who wants to work with dedication and commitment and "who is doing well in life anyway and who is rich". There is also jealousy of the little orphaned patients who receive narcissistic attention from me and become visibly more lively and happier and express delight at seeing me.[7] I am away from East Africa for three months at a time to return to my work in Europe and, each time, I have to leave my little patients behind.

Notes

1 See also Barbara Saegesser, „Gedanken und Anmerkungen zu meiner psychoanalytischen Arbeit in mir fremden Ethnien und am fremden Ort". *Jahrbücher der Kinder und Jugendspezifischen-Psychoanalyse* 2015 and 2016. Brandes und Apsel.

2 I have just learnt that the new Director (as of 2018) of the Kulturforums-/podiums Berlin has declared it a matter of urgency to enlighten visitors about the provenance and acquisition process of the objects exhibited as well as to seek dialogue and take up negotiations with the former owners of the objects concerned.

3 Parallel to the description of the ethnological work with the Dogon, *Phantom Afrika* is interesting to read as the history of ethnological raids: "from rock to rock, from cave to cave, from one holy site to another, everything is being searched, brought out and bundled up" (Leiris 1985, diary entry, 28.8.31) and, "yesterday the Dogon have secretly procured feather costumes for masks, for

Concepts and treatments for psychosomatic patients in East Africa   103

which we had asked them . . . No doubt: our practices have set a precedent: the influence of the European" (12.11.1931).

4 Only when I have worked in a particular place for longer and gained the trust of the people a little, do I hear about the torments of women in harems and in marriages. Many become psychosomatically ill and develop serious depression. Worst affected are the first-chosen wives, because they generally appear to become steadily more unattractive. The husband should not be affected by all these problems of his wives or be exposed to their complaints, because what he does is in keeping with the Quran and therefore legitimate.

5 The more important part of the psychoanalytical frame becomes my inner frame, instead of the outer one, which would be: room, chair, couch etc.

6 As I have described before in several different connections and situations.

7 Today, I realise how very similar mechanisms are beginning to play out in Western European homes and care homes for the elderly and infirm, where residents or patients receive care and attention from external third parties who treat them well, spoil them and appreciate them. Envy and jealousy develop quickly. Besides jealousy, visitors who often visit the homes – not necessarily relatives – can learn too much about unhappy situations going on there and thus become unwelcome with the home management. In East Africa, one female manager told me about such fears. In Western Europe, the home management at times reacts by banning visitors.

Bibliography

Abdel-Samad, H. (2020). *Aus Liebe zu Deutschland: Ein Warnruf*. München: dtv.

Bion, W. R. (2005a). *The Tavistock Seminars*. London: Karnac Books. (German ed.: *Die Tavistock-Seminare*. Frankfurt am Main: Brandes & Apsel, 2007.)

Bion, W. R. (2005b). *The Italian Seminars*. London: Karnac Books. (German ed.: Die italienischen Seminare. Frankfurt am Main: Brandes & Apsel, 2007.)

Freud, Sigmund (1915). *Psychologie des Unbewußten*. Studienausgabe, vol. III. Berlin: S. Fischer Verlag, 1975.

Hirsi Ali, A. (2015). *Reformiert euch! Warum der Islam sich ändern muss*. München: Albrecht Knaus.

Koopmans, Ruud (2019). *Das verfallene Hause des Islams*. München: C. H. Beck.

Klein, Melanie (1962). Neid und Dankbarkeit. In: *Das Seelenleben des Kleinkindes und andere Beiträge zur Psychoanalyse*. Stuttgart: Klett: pp. 177–190.

Klüger, Ruth (2020). *Unterwegs verloren*. München: dtv: pp. 86f.

Leiris, Michel (1985). *Phantom Afrika. Tagebuch einer Expedition von Dakar nach Dschibuti 1931–1933*. First and second parts. Introduction by Hans-Jürgen Heinrichs. Trans. by Rolf Wintermeyer. Frankfurt am Main: Suhrkamp.

Quinodoz, Danielle (2002). *Des mots qui touchent*. Paris: Presses Universitaires de France. (German ed.: *Worte, die berühren*. Frankfurt am Main: Brandes & Apsel.)

Racamier, Paul-Claude (1993). *Le psychanalyste sans divan. La psychanalyse et les institutions de soins psychiatriques*. Bibliothèque Scientifique Payot. Paris: Payot.

Saegesser, Barbara (2012). *Meine psychoanalytische Arbeit in verschiedenen Afrikanischen Ländern*. Basel: Vortrag Psychoanalytisches Seminar.

Saegesser, Barbara (2014). Psychoanalytische Arbeit mit BB's, Kleinkindern und Müttern in unterschiedlichen afrikanischen Ländern (Le travail psychanalytique avec les bébés, des petits enfants et des mères dans divers pays d'Afrique). *Schweizerische Gesellschaft für Psychoanalyse (SGPsa) Bulletin* No. 77 (Spring): 5–13.

Saegesser, Barbara (2015). Psychoanalytische Feldarbeit in ostafrikanischen Städten I. In: Peter Bründl and Carl E. Scheidt (Eds.). *Jahrbuch der Kinder und*

104 *Concepts and treatments for psychosomatic patients in East Africa*

Jugendspezifischen-Psychoanalyse, vol. 4. Frankfurt am Main: Brandes & Apsel: pp. 211–238.

Saegesser, Barbara (2016a). Elternschaft in ostafrikanischen Städten. Psychoanalytische Arbeit mit Müttern, Ersatzmüttern, Vätern und Waisenkindern. In: Peter Bründl and Carl E. Scheidt (Eds.), *Jahrbuch der Kinder und Jugendspezifischen-Psychoanalyse*, vol. 5. Frankfurt am Main: Brandes & Apsel: pp. 269–279.

Saegesser, Barbara (2016b). Un travail psychothérapeutique en marge de ma pratique psychoanalytique et de la culture islamique dans des villes d'Afrique de l'est. (Translation and adaptation of my original manuscript written in German.) Lausanne. *Tribune Psychanalytique* 13.

Saegesser, Barbara (2016c). Eine Skizze psychoanalytiquer Arbeit in ostafrikanischen islamischen Städten. Islamische religiös-weltliche Gesetze und Normen als Basis für Widerstand und Abwehrbewegungen von PatientInnen im Rahmen (situativ angepasster) psychoanalytischer Arbeit. (Zürich*). „A jour"*, 2.

Saegesser, Barbara (2017). „Gleichschwebende" Assessments, ambulatorisches Auswählen und psychoanalytische Kurzpsychotherapie mit adoleszenten Patientinnen im ostafrikanischen Krankensaal. In: Peter Bründl and Fernanda Pedrina (Eds.), *Abklärung – Diagnose – Fallbeschreibung. Forschung und Behandlungsplan. Jahrbuch der Kinder und Jugendspezifischen-Psychoanalyse*, vol. 6. Frankfurt am Main: Brandes & Apsel: pp. 196–215.

Saegesser, Barbara (2018). Psychosomatische Prozesse. In: Peter Bründl and Carl Eduard Scheidt (Eds.). *Jahrbuch der Kinder und Jugendspezifischen-Psychoanalyse*, vol. 7. Frankfurt am Main: Brandes & Apsel: pp. 198–217.

Saegesser, Barbara (2019). Geschlechterdifferenz im Spielraum. In: Peter Bründl and Helene Timmermann (Eds.), *Jahrbuch der Kinder und Jugendspezifischen-Psychoanalyse*, vol. 8. Frankfurt am Main: Brandes & Apsel: pp. 254–279.

Schreiber, Constantin (2020). *Kinder der Koran. Was muslimische Schüler lernen*. Berlin: Ullstein.

11 Free ambulatory choice of patients in the main room of the women's station

My psychoanalytic work in hospitals shows in many respects little agreement with classical European hospital and classical, conventional, psychoanalytic work. Without my psychoanalytic working and teaching in Europe over many years, and without my extensive active and passive experience and self-experience with my psychoanalytic concepts and models, I would not be able to work in East African hospitals and in psychiatric rooms in the way I have done. The shortness of time available for my psychotherapeutic work with one female patient at a time (often in the company of two to three female family members) is dictated and structured by institutional processes and is also culturally determined. Of course, my time is always restricted also as a result of my stays in the country being only temporary. By "culturally determined", I mean various things. In most East African ethnicities, the lengths of relationships with extended family are unlimited in time. Medical or other therapeutic courses of treatment on the other hand, for example those provided by healers, usually last for a short period only. For most treatments, just one to two sessions are required but a prospective view of time in the sense of forward planning tends not to be part of the way of life for East African people. The reasons for this seem various, and I cannot go into them here in detail. The uncertainty, abrupt changes and instability experienced in reality constantly run parallel to the phantasmatic condition of a good way for life being planned by the family, and this projected safety is fundamentally rooted in religion. The basis for forward planning, decision making and the provision of safety, stability and reliability in life is firmly anchored in religion, in religious scriptures and doctrine.

When I return to my work in Europe, I generally do so for three months at a time. Some patients bridge this three-month pause in their psychotherapy by waiting and, afterwards, come back to continue with it. This is mainly the case with people who have an above-average level of education. They seem to be able to cope with time planning and postponing dates into the future.

As a rule, the time available for carrying out psychotherapeutic work with patients is tight. The allocated two to three sessions are time-wise,

DOI: 10.4324/9781003451587-11

106 *Free ambulatory choice of patients in the women's station*

and often also regarding the venue, not firmly prearranged. Once patients have overcome their initial scepticism and resistance to therapy, they utilise their sessions intensively and fruitfully. Above all, patients in Psychiatry and those who have been referred to me from elsewhere tend to begin their psychotherapeutic conversations with the attitude: I am fine, there's nothing wrong with me. In the regions of East Africa where I work, this initial resistance has, as I see it, its roots in Quranic beliefs (Saegesser 2016a, 2016b). In the general hospital, I hardly ever encounter such an attitude of resistance. Here, the priority lies with the physical pain.

Once the scepticism and resistance towards therapeutic intervention have faded away, it becomes evident that, fortunately, the patients are devoid of any pre-scientific pre-knowledge about psychoanalytic psychotherapy, or psychotherapy per se. In Western societies, such pre-knowledge can crystallise into psychic movements resembling initial scepticism and resistance towards therapy. In this sense, many patients I work with in East African hospitals are psychoanalytically and psychotherapeutically "unspoiled", maybe similarly to the way many patients in the early 1900s during Freud's times began therapy in an "unspoiled" state. The influence of possible former therapeutic intervention, of self-help literature, tips and hints garnered from popular TV and radio programmes, and so on, is completely absent. The rational and emotional processes and situations present in unadulterated form, and the patients work undistractedly on the central issues that make them suffer. With my patients, I express myself in simple terms. I resist offering complicated explanations (which might invite resistance), and I choose words that move and touch (Quinodoz 2002). What I mean by speaking in a clear way and by addressing latent issues in an unveiled way can be seen in my vignette where I describe my work with Ne, a severely emaciated anorexic patient about 13 years old.

Much of what I do in the hospital in seeking for clarifications, selecting patients and the treatments I choose, may be reminiscent of Bion's considerations in his Italian and Tavistock Seminars (Bion 2005a, 2005b). He writes about how the spoken language does not necessarily help us in furthering our understanding of our patients' mental processes. We see our patients vis-à-vis as whole human beings, also physically. We do so by their rhythmic or repetitive movements or by their inhibition, by the sound and melody of their voices, by the nature of the expression of their eyes and by the feel of their handshakes. How little grammatical accuracy in spoken language actually matters, I have frequently realised in my psychoanalytic work in East African institutions over the years.

Working with interpreters

Working with interpreters is always also a restrictive experience. They are likely to distort the actual patient–psychotherapist process but, at the same

Free ambulatory choice of patients in the women's station   107

time, also act as buffers against unconscious movements. Interpreters and their translations inadvertently claim a part of the patient's transference onto their psychotherapist, a part technically seen as appertaining to the patient. Our capacity to remain open to our patients and to be able to give them fully narcissistic support is, especially with severely traumatised patients, of primary importance. This capacity is invariably curtailed when collaborating with interpreters, however well-qualified and expert they may be.

In the East African environment, this third party is likely to share a similar ethnic background to that of the patient, a background very different from that of the "white woman", and therefore tends to want to put a "better", more familiar and more "accurate" slant on the proceedings. This distorts the actual or shared fantasised process developing between the patient and his psychoanalyst. In order to be able to approach a patient, a varied and specific use of language is essential. Such specific use of language is equally essential for a patient to be able to be life-narcissistically touched. Awareness of this is frequently lacking, also in a professional environment.

I speak of my free choice of patients and included in this are the thoughts and comments I have so far developed and described. Now I describe how I seek patients in a hospital station and how the first contacts can be. The psychotherapeutic conversations following later mostly confirm my initial, hypothetical diagnosis.

My present approach in the choice of patients for psychotherapeutic work

Babies, children, street boys – selecting patients from various groups and working with them psychotherapeutically has been and remains the centre of my working in foreign territories ever since I began to do so in East Africa, from the north to the most southern states. I did not choose this approach freely, it was unavoidable, since in East Africa psychological or psychoanalytic thinking, considering, looking, understanding and diagnosing were, and still are, practically unknown. In order to find my patients, I stand or sit before mixed groups – in orphanages, in homes for street children, in international orphanage organisations, in rooms for pre- and post-operative women, in psychiatric and general hospitals.

In one quite large hospital, my work is often similar to that of a first responder in an emergency. I find around 15–20 patients lying in beds standing in a disorderly fashion all over a large, open room. Here, I choose my patients. In contrast to many Western European institutions, I am only rarely directly asked anything by doctors, unless a patient becomes extremely difficult. Otherwise, I go slowly and alone through the different stations (maternity, neonatal and children, general medicine, psychiatric rooms). I observe, consider, study, listen, smell. I register movements and contours, also culture-specific ones – e.g. a patient tied to a bed. If I come across something that falls outside the set of this place's culture-specific norms which I have worked out for myself, then I first observe and consider the situation from a certain spatial distance.

When I enter a hospital, the first thing I do is establish whether it is in what counts as a relatively normal, average state of calm, or in a state of unrest and turbulence. This then forms the normative basis from which I begin my choice. I look at the room as I would look at a new landscape I have come across. I look around for a bit, proceed on my way, look a bit more, may feel surprised, may not see clearly, would like to have a closer look at something, I am unsure, keep looking back at something, look away, might prefer not to have seen something, would rather look at something else more carefully. Something conspicuous, something of a certain shape or colour attracts my eye: like some bushes, trees, hills, fields, tended land, neglected spaces, patches of old snow, or the dry stubble in a field of maize. I register the seasons, whether someone has looked after the fields. Do they look cared for, neglected, left to rot? How does this part of the world smell? What does it sound like? What, for me, is it that sticks out especially?

An illustrative example is when, dreamily gazing at and gazing through things, I notice a patient sitting cross-legged on her bed. The fact that she is sitting cross-legged is not immediately obvious to me, and the significance of it I only realise later. I first register her sitting there like a kind of monument placed on a bed – a pretty face, fairly wide in proportion, seemingly smiling. She faces the other patients' beds, silently, not really seeing them, with no perceptible physical movement. She is wrapped in a blanket, and her head is covered. Her body is a sort of mass, practically without contours, except for the fact that it seems to become somewhat unnaturally narrower towards the top. As I keep looking, I notice something discreetly elegant about her, something rhythmic – despite the lack of discernible physical contours. Her neck, arms, hands, chest, stomach, legs and feet flow over and into each other, forming large shapes.

The patient, I will call her B, seems serene, friendly. She has a beautiful face, is attractively dressed in black combined with colours. She continues to sit there cross-legged on her old iron bed, Buddha-like, a figurine. She radiates a sense of harmony as well as of contrasts. She appears silent. There are no other patients or care staff in her vicinity despite the fact that she exudes something subtle and select, maybe also something mysterious. She appears motionless and a little static perhaps. She looks, but she doesn't seem to see. She troubles me. What is it about her? What is it that this perhaps motionless girl moves within me?

At first glance, there seems nothing wrong, yet there is also something not quite right which I can neither find out nor define a little. I decide to return to her later on and shall write about the psychotherapeutic conversations I have with her.

Free ambulatory choice of patients in the women's station   109

Another encounter that falls outside the standard of my norms I use is with a young girl, her face bathed in sweat, being physically propped up and supported especially around the head. The girl is jerking from one side to the other side as if shaken by force from the inside. Standing with her are two to three probably related people. The girl's name is Ka, and her story also follows later in this chapter.

Also in the same room, there is a little girl, totally emaciated, skeletal, who watches me. A woman sits on her bed and I shall say more about her later.

Much of what is "abnormal" I recognise in comparison with what is classed as normal: calm versus unrest; static versus in motion; a direct look at me versus an empty look not focused on anything, or the avoidance of a direct look at me. My process of looking is the process of interpreting the world of a hospital. All this is not dissimilar to the approach I adopt with patients whom I meet for the first time, or meet anew, in my European practice.

My way of looking at these moments is dreamy, a reverie, a preconscious kind of look at the hospital room which absorbs and differentiates till it catches on something, becomes clearer, more conscious, transforms into consciousness. Dreamy looking results in diffuse realisations; introjections and projections play together. Similar to creative thinking, creative writing and painting, reverie as a type of experience and a way of experiencing in a wider context should, in my view, be able to rest on much of the already psychoanalytically experienced, not only on the one-to-one relationship between mother and child or between psychoanalyst and patient. It seems to me important, therefore, to have seen much, heard much, smelt much, experienced much, in order to approach a hospital situation in an only minimally delimited way, and to later diagnostically structure these experiences and introduce them into the clinical process, and transform the status quo. For this psychoanalytic theory of recognition and psychoanalytic practice of recognition, W. R. Bion's thoughts are seminal. His suggestion of transforming reverie in such a way that enables us to enter formalised short results into the grid he has devised points to a combinatory transformation of the emotional irrational into the rational. He attempts to introduce a check for what is being recognised through reverie, a post-check so to speak. As far as I am aware, W. R. Bion makes no further mention of this in his later work.

Of course, encounters with potential patients on the basis of my free selection of patients in an East African hospital are different compared to when I am asked to visit a patient in a specific room and given information about this patient prior to our first meeting. In the latter case, I meet the patient not on a "fresh" and "uncontaminated" basis but on a basis distorted by prior knowledge. I invariably memorise what I have heard about the patient before and this disturbs, or sullies, my dreamy perception, my looking, my smelling, my listening and so on. My perception is sometimes reduced, if not blocked by knowledge – at least initially. Despite

110 *Free ambulatory choice of patients in the women's station*

that, however, I often succeed in regaining access to my dreamy contemplation and perception.

This is the case with patient Na. I am told that she does not eat, drink or speak. I put this information aside. I notice how she slowly and repeatedly strokes parts of her body: first her breasts, then her stomach, then the pubic area.

Having described my initially dreamy perception of the hospital room, I will now show how I deepen the insights gained with the help of patients, family members, the helping people and the patient's medical information. I will also demonstrate how I work psychoanalytically with my various patients and, specifically, what I do psychoanalytically-therapeutically here in East Africa. By my working here, I do not mean speaking in the local language (Swahili) but my attempt to take into account my understanding of the most important cultural aspects involved, to incorporate them into my working process and to integrate them in the therapeutic process. Part of this expansion of my psychoanalytic-psychotherapeutic model in the East African context is physical touching. Physical contact can play an important role in a familial environment, but, interestingly, not necessarily outside this environment in a public space. Of course, the question arises where and how to touch. I proceed carefully, as I would like my touching not to be perceived as pushy or intrusive, but as calming or as revitalising. I mostly touch, where possible, a foot (Saegesser 2015, 2016a). These touches may last longer or be short, and are always as light as a feather. Where a family member, predominantly the mother, is particularly needy, physically and mentally exhausted and tense, I gently stroke her back. Sometimes I do so also before leaving a patient. In a hospital setting, touching seems even more natural, it happens as a matter of course. In East African psychotherapy, if it takes place outside the hospital building, I generally desist from making physical contact, as this is a different situation to the one where patients are lying in the hospital. One exception would be extremely deprived patients who are possibly also suffering from a mild learning disability (see Saegesser 2016b).

In the hospital, the therapeutic processes I initiate with young people are invariably always also family-related and include mothers, grandmothers, sisters and aunts. The family relationship is per se the most important relationship in a female human being's life. The exception is where a woman has flouted one or several predominantly religious laws or stands accused of having done so (possibly without factual evidence) and is being, as a result, excluded from the family bond and also from socio-cultural relations. She has to stand out, because she becomes ignored and put outside her former social relations and groups.

Of course, female family members react entirely differently to my work: partly interested, partly half-frightened, partly reticent, dismissive and so on. Were I a male psychotherapist, I would immediately enjoy more initial

Free ambulatory choice of patients in the women's station 111

trust, respect and confidence in my abilities. Men are the dominant members of society in this culture. Yet, women are gaining increasing access to education and further training and can now work as, for example, medical doctors. Rivalries amongst women are, as in many places, present here also. Naturally, I am made to feel this as well. My white skin colour is at times seen as that of the former colonists. These colonists, however, also possessed specifically different and vital knowledge. Healers, too, have such specifically different knowledge and, further, have the ability to exorcise evil spirits or Djins, seen as the causes of illness and disease. (Evil spirits are named differently according to regions.) It is possible that patients' relatives at times also see some of this in me and in my actions. They have hope, but at the same time feel a little apprehensive, unsure, frightened on account of the new, the incomprehensible, which I supposedly and yet obviously introduce.

Vignettes

Vignette 1: female patient Na

I approach Na, put specific information I have heard about her aside and go closer, taking her in as a whole human being: her body, her movements, the sounds she makes and her smell. I look in the direction where something is happening, where she is doing something to herself, where she is pointing out, to me and to everyone else, something different to what has been discussed during this morning's briefing and ostensibly alarming: she is stroking herself, across her whole body, especially her breasts and the pubic area.

The young woman is around 16 years old and has been assessed by the hospital as having a mild learning disability. At home, she performs her duties independently. She has an uncle with whom she gets on especially well, says her mother. I ask her, after having introduced myself, whether it would be possible for this uncle, with whom the patient gets on so well, to come to the hospital. It transpires after some discussion that the "uncle" is not a relative but a neighbour (it is culturally fairly common to call neighbours uncles, or aunts mothers). Apparently, the uncle has only just today, the day of Na's admission to hospital, gone away somewhere. It was not possible to get him to come to the hospital. This is strange, I think to myself. What is happening between this man and this adolescent, mildly learning-disabled girl?

Na is lying quietly on her bed. I notice a little resistance. She has her eyes closed and is throwing herself from side to side. Then, for a short moment, she lies still, almost frozen, only to then resume her frantic twisting. I assume that now she has realised my presence. I am standing at the bottom of the iron bedstead and watch what is happening with her almost

112   *Free ambulatory choice of patients in the women's station*

naked body, or what she is doing with it. I also want to see whether she will now show interest in me or not, whether she will look at me. I get the impression that she does so at times: for split seconds, surreptitiously; or for longer, with a somewhat blank gaze. After a while – I proceed slowly and calmly – I begin to speak her name, softly, quietly, melodiously and with a long-drawn-out vowel sound, never statically, stiffly or aggressively. Mother and sister are probably a little puzzled by what is going on. One by one, onlookers appear, relatives of other patients, members of the care staff. Many evidently realise that something is happening that does not happen every day in this room. I have to send them away and ask for a screen.

I try to touch very lightly one of the patient's feet. She allows this to happen, and I continue to sing her name quietly and at intervals now, while I cup my hands around her feet and slowly stroke them. The patient intermittently calms down for short spells, then, with a start, her movements flare up again. Her right hand is bandaged with a piece of cloth. She opens her eyes a little, only to a small slit, and looks at me and suddenly she rears up and pulls with all her might at that bandaged right hand which it seems cannot be moved. Only then do I realise that she has been tied to the bedstead by that hand. The supposed bandage is a restraint and I ask why she has been tied down. If she is not restrained, she runs off all over the ward, from bed to bed, and upsets everything, I am told.

I notice again that if the patient is lying quietly, she keeps touching her breasts, stroking them, then moves her hands across her stomach and begins to stroke herself in the pubic area as well. I ask once more whether the "uncle" – the neighbour – could not come to the hospital. Again, I am told no. So, I begin to ask about him, as I suspect that Na may have been sexually in contact with him or even abused. She touches herself in those areas of her body where sexual activity takes place. She is adolescent and mildly learning-disabled. This can be an ideal condition to fall victim to sexual abuse.

Again, a crowd has assembled around us. I try, using European manners, to shoo them away a little and to calm the situation down, to create a calmer atmosphere. Suddenly, the mother becomes active and she pulls at the sheets, smooths out creases, starts putting extra bits of cloth on the sheet. She seems very worried, and at the same time, it seems to me, full of suppressed anger because her daughter causes her so much work and worry. I seem to detect a mother–daughter conflict as an additional deeper problem. The daughter tries to loosen her ties with her mother, possibly also with the "help" of this so-called uncle. And somehow symbolically, the mother ties her daughter to the iron bedstead. At this moment the priority is not speaking, drinking or eating. Too much else is happening and Na is expressing other needs urgently and impressively. I am still in the process of singing her name and stroking her feet. At the moment it would be futile to do anything about the restraint around her hand, although

Free ambulatory choice of patients in the women's station 113

inwardly I am upset and angry, also as a form of counter-transference. I know that there are no cultural norms that denounce the use of such restraints. There are also none that denounce physical punishment of children and wives and women. I must be careful not to affront the mother as she, before I arrived, had already indicated that she wanted to take her daughter home again. Many patients distrust hospitals. They likely have already consulted a traditional healer or intend to do so in the future when they believe that an evil spirit, a Djin, is at the root of their illness or that of a relative.

Despite all this, I do not forget that Na should at least drink a little to secure her physical survival, since the hospital has to save on infusions. (The financial situation of the hospital is dire, not to say catastrophic: not enough medication, a lack of specific medication, not enough oxygen bottles and so on.)

After a longer interval, around 20 minutes perhaps, I ask the mother to pour some water into a cup and to hand it to me. I remain at the bottom of the bed and indicate to Na that she should sit up. I play a mother-and-child game with her (a Western European game, not knowing if and how this would work in this present environment). I pretend Na is a small child and that I am drinking a little from the cup and then, I take the cup to her mouth, and she drinks a little herself. I repeat this sequence three or four times. Drinking in this hot climate is probably the most important act of survival. Now, the first step on the path to survival has been taken. The mother reacts with slight relaxation and a little smile in my direction.

Once Na's temperature has been taken and other checks made, it transpires that the patient is suffering from a severe bladder infection. This, too, might be indicative of sexual abuse.

Having been psychotherapeutically and medically treated, Na becomes calmer. She drinks, eats and at times dozes off. When she opens her eyes, she looks into my eyes, and the resistance I felt at the beginning seems to have gone. Her hand restraint has been removed. My mainly psychotherapeutic procedure for when I visit Na at least twice a day remains as described earlier: the melodious calling out of her name, the touching and stroking of her feet, eye contact, exchange of looks, and of course my comprehensive holding can introduce something positive to her narcissism. Almost all women and patients suffer from a severe lack of narcissistic positive affection and positive gratitude, and this lack begins possibly in utero, by birth or early childhood.

Two days later, I find Na again tied to the bedstead, this time by both hands. I fail to notice this immediately since everything is concealed again under sheets and bits of cloth. Mother and sister complain that if Na is not tied down, she is too restless. Na rears up and tries to pull herself free just like on the first day. She refuses to drink or eat. I work with her in the same way I have been doing till now. After she has calmed down, I begin again with the mother-and-child drinking game: first I pretend to take a sip, then

114 *Free ambulatory choice of patients in the women's station*

she actually drinks a little. If she stops too soon, I simulate a couple more sips, then she takes the cup, and so on. She has started eating again, the bladder infection has improved.

Five days later, Na seems a little bit quieter and she looks at me trustingly, maybe even a little longingly. I am alone with her and we work together via non-verbal exchange. She drinks and eats and I remain uncertain as to whether Na actually has the power of speech.

Mother and sister are absent for the moment. Na expresses herself effectively, without words, and I notice that she really is getting better, both physically and mentally. Our psychotherapeutic collaboration is disrupted the moment the mother returns. She appears happy and says she may take Na home today. Then, the mother begins again, like on the previous days, frantically to pack, to unpack, to pack, to unpack. She works at lightning speed, removes something quickly, lays something down, wants to do something with the patient, tugs at her and the patient of course again refuses to eat or drink as well as to take her medicine. The mother tells her off and I try to stop the mother. She makes me angry because she cannot leave her daughter alone, keeps constantly tugging at her, pinching her, is incessantly in the process of "doing and fussing". Na must, according to her mother, take the tablets with some water and she refuses. She wants to take them without water – probably so as to resist anything the mother decides and orders her to do. She then accepts a little water from me. First, she picks something off the rim of the cup, something that obviously disgusts her, then she takes her tablet with some water. Interestingly, the mother had, before passing the cup to Na, already performed the same gesture on the rim of the cup as her daughter: desperately, something had to be removed! This shows just how closely together lie Na's demonstrative rejection of her mother on the one hand – her desire to separate from her mother – and her desire to identify with and imitate her on the other. From a psychoanalytical point of view, identification is also a contributory factor in suppressing or splitting off aggression.

The situation is, of course, not simple, as the mother is now the wicked one from whom Na wants to separate, but at the same time also the so-called good, benevolent one. Once they are home, I can no longer act as this third, auxiliary object that can help with the splitting off or, later, with the building of a separating bridge between mother and daughter.

Na slowly gets out of bed, and I say goodbye to her. She appears calm, reflective, a little depressed. Immediately, the mother interferes again and tugs at "her girl".

During the time of these psychotherapeutic treatments or non-verbal conversations, my diagnosis of a separation conflict has reaffirmed itself. The diagnostic hypothesis of sexual abuse remains intact, too.

Of course, what I have been able to achieve with this patient in my non-verbal exchanges with her could be seen, in "European" terms, as an emergency intervention. I was unable to do more for cultural reasons.

Free ambulatory choice of patients in the women's station 115

I would have had time available and could have worked with the patient for an additional week, but where and when? In the psychiatric rooms, where I also work, this would easily have been possible, given its isolated locality. People here, however, as is so often the case not only in East African cities, shy away from psychiatric clinics – they prefer not to visit them and never to have been there. The attitude persists that attending or staying at a psychiatric clinic is something to be ashamed of.

Vignette 2: female patient Ka

I have already mentioned patient Ka earlier. I notice her from a distance, shortly before leaving one evening. Her face is bathed in sweat, and she seems to be thrown from side to side as if by an inner force. Her bed is surrounded by women who try to hold and support her, especially around her head. Hysterical convulsions is what goes through my mind. Here in East Africa, I sometimes come across psychological illnesses or processes which in central Western European societies present in weakened or changed forms only. It seems that Ka is today suffering from the same condition as yesterday. I read her medical information, which tells me little, and I try to talk to the care women (a challenge linguistically) to find out whether Ka has been seen by a doctor. Yes, a doctor has been to see her, I am told, and, apparently, he wanted to do a puncture, but the needle was unsuitable and broke. This is what I believe I can make out from what I have been told. I purposely describe this problem of uncertainty I encounter with regard to what I am told, to give a clear picture of my working conditions. I now try to work out with mother and aunt what happened to her daughter and when, and what had happened before then. The daughter was at home, I am told, then went to her aunt in the neighbouring house where there is a television. There were several people sitting in front of the television. Then, the patient went out to buy crisps for everyone and everybody took from these crisps. The patient returned to the mother and, afterwards, went back to the aunt's house to spend the night there. In the morning, she could not rise, was restless and kept twisting in bed and she was bathed in sweat. I am being told this story in great detail, and there seems to be relief about the fact that there is someone interested to patiently and attentively listen. This is already the third day that the patient has been ill. I ask a few clarifying questions about drugs, alcohol and tablets, what it is she has eaten and so on. Nothing of all this seems to be at the root of the problem. Fortunately, an experienced medical colleague appears, who has his shift on this Saturday and with whom I am able to discuss the situation. He checks the physical condition of the patient. This shows that the patient, when very directly addressed by a man, reacts a little, even tries to speak, and with great effort tries to look at him and to move her arms and legs. It now becomes clearer – this is not about convulsions and also not about severe

116 *Free ambulatory choice of patients in the women's station*

cerebral damage. What is she suffering from, we ask ourselves. Might she have been stung by a scorpion? No, my colleague replies, less likely stung by a scorpion than perhaps bitten by a snake. We then check the soles of the patient's feet and, indeed, find bite marks. Would the hospital have a general antidote? No, first one would have to know exactly what kind of snake it was. I ask him to send for a surgical colleague. He does so, and does so again in the evening because I, before leaving the hospital, go to see the patient and learn that nothing has been arranged from the surgical side and I ask him again by telephone. He promises he will urge the matter on.

The following morning, Ka seems to have improved a tiny bit, but she is still not at all well. Obviously, no surgeon has been to see her. She seems a little less tortured and the atmosphere is somewhat more relaxed. I try to calm Ka down a bit more by applying the melodious ritual of singing her name. I myself remain very worried about her condition and upset because of the inadequate medical attention she is receiving. I think to myself: of course, she is only a woman and by this fact alone stands a lesser chance of receiving reliable and state-of-the-art medical care. Accompanied by a young female doctor, I go in search of a surgeon who can attend to the patient. It has now been four days since she has been poisoned. Eventually, an assistant hesitantly applies some cuts to the patient's foot. A carer says to me grumpily that there's nothing coming out. I reply that the poison has had three to four days to spread throughout her whole body. This was my last day of my present spell of working at this hospital. I do not know how the patient progressed after that and I asked the medical doctor in charge by email to pay special attention to patient Ka and to examine and look after her well. I never received an answer back.

The case of my patient Ka took its course in the opposite direction: from a psychosomatic diagnosis to a somatic one. Had I not noticed patient Ka, she would have continued to lie in that hospital without diagnosis and without medical care, and she would have been entirely left alone in her acute state of poisoning.

The obvious and severe physical symptoms of Ka's poisoning were clear indices of her suffering. Yet, no member of the hospital staff reacted unprompted and effectively. It remained unclear what had happened to Ka before her illness and nobody was interested in finding this out, as if questions about the cause of the problem and the problem itself were difficult to work out and clear up. Was there no interest because the situation was too unfamiliar and too time consuming to deal with? Even if the cause of the illness was almost certainly known (snake poison), it was evidently hardly possible to treat it. Might the fact that it was a female patient rather than a male patient have played a role? Or, because it would have been too much of a challenge to do "this, that or the other"? Ka clearly only received any medical care at all on account of my intervention and this is an example that highlights some of the reasons why my work is meaningful

Free ambulatory choice of patients in the women's station   117

and important. It is for such reasons also that at times this kind of work is almost unbearable to sustain. The impulse is there to just give up. Many do give up. What are their reasons? Are they not interested, do they feel helpless, powerless, do they feel they cannot apply logical reasoning and draw logical conclusions in many of the situations they encounter? Can they not? Do they not want to?

Vignette 3: anorexic patient Ne

During my extremely short period of working with patient Ne, it becomes clear to me how openly I speak with hospital patients, depending on the situation, and how openly I interpret, since I have learnt that this way often fruitfully and quickly leads to psychic changes in the patient. I notice this patient especially because she hardly occupies any space in her iron bed and is lying there like a small, neglected bundle of bones. By her bedside sits a woman with a strikingly clear and agreeable countenance. I approach the bed. I have noticed the girl looking at me several times from a distance, watching what I am doing in the large room. The girl speaks Swahili while her companion, whom I am told is the mother, speaks in English to me. I ask a few questions. It interests me to know whether this is the first time that the little girl has become so emaciated and ill. No, I am told, this happens from time to time. Ne refuses to eat or drink and loses weight dramatically, but she has never been as bad as this. I then ask whether Ne's companion has an explanation for this, and whether she is the mother of the girl. No, she says, she cannot explain why this happens, and she is not the mother of the girl but the sister of the mother. She says she knows nothing, and I wonder whether something serious, traumatic might have happened to the girl. I am told that the mother of the girl had died immediately after the birth of Ne, and that she had been cared for in three different places before she went to live with her aunt. While I am speaking, the girl studies my face attentively. From what I am learning now, and from what I have read of the medical information, she is 13 years old. She has been prescribed folic acid, and a blood transfusion is planned also. A member of the care team comes to stand beside me, and I ask her whether nobody has mentioned anorexia. No, she says, and she asks what anorexia is. I explain it to her in brief terms. I also mention that a person who refuses nutrition may, without really being aware of this themselves, harbour a wish to die. I have to be careful with the term "suicide", as Islam forbids suicide. I also explain to the aunt what I think about the girl's illness and ask her whether she would translate for the patient. She agrees instantly. Speaking with this severely emaciated, sick girl, who looks at me with a serious and very sad expression on her face, I tell her roughly the following: You are extremely weak at the moment and also seriously ill. You are so ill that you now have to lie in hospital. Your aunt tells me that from time to time you make yourself weak by not eating and by hardly drinking anything and until now, there

118 *Free ambulatory choice of patients in the women's station*

has always been some changing point at which you have started to eat again. This time round, it seems to be different. If one stops eating completely, one might think, for example, that in this way one can die. And if one thinks like that, one does so because at times one might prefer to be dead rather than alive, because one's own life and the environment in which one lives are all so full of pain and sorrow. (I explain these things using the neutral "one" on purpose, leaving it up to the patient whether she wishes to apply what I am saying to her own life and her own context or not.) I believe that this is what happens with you sometimes. You have never known your mother properly. After your birth, she died immediately. (Here, unlike I would do in a Western European environment, I desist from touching upon the problem of a possible guilt complex in this connection – personal guilt about the death of the mother.) You long for your mother and you think that if she were here, many things would be better for you and your life, and you want to be with her. She is dead, and I can imagine that you have already had the thought that if you were dead as well, you would be able to be with her. Well, if you really want to be dead, then it is right if you continue to refuse to eat. If you do not really want to be dead, then you have no alternative but to start to eat and drink. You must eat and drink every day, and several times a day. And what do you say now? Do you really want to die? The girl looks at me for a long time, quietly. Then she shakes her head and begins to eat. I see this and support this and say: "Tomorrow I shall come back to see you and to see how you are doing."

Here, I interpret for her in clear, blunt terms her wish to starve herself to death: so that, as a dead person, she can be with her mother again, be reunited with her, in the hope that everything would be better and alright again. I also tell her that if she really wishes to die, then she is on the right track by refusing to eat. If, however, she wants to live, she must eat, and eat a lot. These are extremely confronting, open interventions. At the same time, they are deep interpretations. I thereby risk that the patient may close up. From the beginning, I did not have this impression here. On the other hand, we can never know what patients may make of what we say to them, what may develop from it or not develop from it. The situation may slip into the negative, harden up and become sterile.

The following morning – it is the last day before my departure – I return to see Ne. Her aunt sits by her bedside and helps her to eat. Since leaving her the day before, the patient apparently has been eating and drinking repeatedly and in good portions. The aunt is relieved and glad. The patient looks at me, seems reassured, and I stand by her bedside and stroke her back, which she has turned towards me while her aunt helps her to eat. Now she stops eating and the aunt asks why. The girl replies: "I don't want to eat so that the woman will continue to stroke me and not stop with it." The aunt understands this and does not urge her to eat at this moment. I continue to stroke Ne's bony, completely emaciated little

Free ambulatory choice of patients in the women's station   119

back. In this way, I am stroking her physical deficiency while at the same time also stroking her inner, mental deficiency, too.

Vignette 4: female patient B

Patient B appears to me from a distance like a Buddha sculpture. In direct contact with her, much happens between her and me in accordance with this complex image that I have created of her. She has a restrained, yet inviting smile, but she remains silent in every respect, and she is not obviously hostile in her silence – more reclusive, closed up. I ask whether I may sit down. There is room on the edge of the bed as she occupies part of the bed only, but she may feel threatened by someone sitting too close to her, she may tense up. She does not react, so I take the risk and I tentatively try to ascertain whether she speaks perhaps English. Very little, she says and then, silence. I remain sitting where I am and try to bear and go with her inner resistance, myself sitting still, hardly moving. After about ten minutes, I leave her, facing her and in a friendly way saying goodbye. I turn my attention to another patient. From afar, I see how patient B constantly follows me with her eyes and observes me.

From the medical information, I learn that B's right arm had to be amputated some time ago. At the moment, she is in hospital for checks on a suspected new outbreak of cancerous growth on her body. I am shocked as I read this, and at the same time much is explained of the image I have of the patient and her particular way of veiling herself: her inertia, for example, may have to do with her amputated arm, her shame and fear of death, and possibly also the erroneous idea of revitalising the cancer through body movements. Shame and fear of death make her become inert in an "outwardly friendly" way. B seems at first sight not at all grim or completely desperate. She tries to show herself as content and serene, like a wise Buddha that has accepted and is resigned to his fate. And, as I understand it, she wishes to appear attentive, while inwardly feeling withdrawn from the world and trapped. This seemingly serene image, at peace with all personal predicaments, and this resistance against destructive awfulness, often present with Central European adolescents. With B, her motives are possibly a little different: religious influence (the Quran), religious dictate may effect a change of this withdrawal in the opposite direction or, expressed in Winnicott's diagnostic concept, effect the partial construction of a false self. The Quran says what Allah decides and decrees is right and good (Saegesser 2016a, 2016b).

I am now often with B, who has been spending the last three days sitting cross-legged on her sickbed whiling her time away. In the end, she receives her medical results: the test results on the suspected cancerous growth prove positive. Her cancer is back with renewed virulence.

I speak little and the contents hardly change: how dreadful and hard the loss of her arm is, how difficult the wait is for a new, specified diagnosis, how terrible and cruel this new cancer diagnosis is for her. I desist out of

120 *Free ambulatory choice of patients in the women's station*

consideration for her religious beliefs the interpretation of how desperately unfair it must seem that the cancer has hit her for a second time. My other interventions are already somewhat risky. B has developed some trust in me, and I notice that she is glad when I am near her, but at the same time her deep despair becomes evident. Now and again, she whines, quietly and for a long time and this opening up, her despair that now comes to the surface, has the effect that the care persons are more responsive and empathetic towards her. She no longer has the status "bed XY". Patients with whom I work are often suddenly perceived differently by their environment, they are invested with interest and as a result treated better – as long as no feelings of jealousy arise. Jealousy and rivalry often play their role, be it in respect of patients who can work with me, be it in respect of the seemingly magical powers of the white woman doctor. The term psychotherapy and the profession of psychotherapist are unknown concepts.

Of course, I also meet patients who prefer not to work with me. Besides the narcissistic or the hysterical accentuation, many other aspects come into play: the cultural preference of men, the cultural preference of non-white Muslim medical carers, the feelings of boiling rivalry in respect of a white woman esteemed and appreciated by others for her personality, which seemingly is strong and has been experienced as helpful. Of course, as with every psychotherapeutic intervention, there is the more or less openly displayed psychic resistance which precedes and/or accompanies it. For effective psychoanalytic treatment of this, however, too little time is allocated to me and my patients by the hospitals I work in.

Bibliography

Bion, Wilfred R. (2005a). *The Tavistock Seminars*. London: Karnac Books.
Bion, Wilfred R. (2005b). *The Italian Seminars*. London: Karnac Books.
Quinodoz, Danielle (2002). *Des mots qui touchent*. Paris: Presses Universitaires de France.
Saegesser, Barbara (2015). Psychoanalytische Feldarbeit in Ostafrikanischen Städten. In: Peter Bründl and Carl E. Scheidt (Eds.), *Spätadoleszenz: Identitätsprozesse und kultureller Wandel. Jahrbuch der Kinder- und Jugendlichen-Psychoanalyse*, vol. 4. Frankfurt am Main: Brandes und Apsel: pp. 211–238.
Saegesser, Barbara (2016a). Psychoanalytische Feldarbeit in Ostafrikanischen Städten II. Elternschaft in ostafrikanischen Städten. In: Peter Bründl and Carl E. Scheidt (Eds.), *Jahrbuch der Kinder- und Jugendlichen-Psychoanalyse*, vol. 5. Frankfurt am Main: Brandes und Apsel: pp. 269–279.
Saegesser, Barbara (2016b). Eine Skizze psychoanalytischer Arbeit in ostafrikanischen islamischen Städten. Islamische religiös-weltliche Gesetze und Normen als Basis für Widerstand und Abwehrbewegungen von PatientInnen im Rahmen (situativ angepasster) psychoanalytischer Arbeit. *„A jour"*, 2.

12 What is it that initiates inner and outer psychic change? What initiates a transformation process?

To conclude, I come again to the meta-psychoanalytic question that can be put to my described specific East African psychoanalytic thinking and acting (talking is also a form of acting): What is effective, what reaches the baby, the younger and the oldest East African patient, and what makes them develop in a relatively short space of time and initiates transformative impulses to unfold?

There are probably many factors, at the surface and in the background, that play a role in the special status that attaches to my person. I cannot know these precisely, but I can fantasise about them: I am a white, foreign woman (in Swahili: Mzungu), a non-Muslim, usually moving around the hospital rooms without male company; someone who tends to approach patients unexpectedly to talk to them, someone about whom people talk and tell perhaps news and curious stories, someone who is said to have healing powers and who has cured the sick in a new way and so on. All these attributes, and probably many more, are becoming more and more concrete in different ways, depending on the patients involved, and partially colour my reputation, positively or negatively. I think that such phantasmatic visualisations of my position in the East African environment are not that different from the strange fantasies and imaginations which East African people have about healers in common with doctors. Healers must above all be capable of exorcising evil spirits from the bodies of the possessed.

If I concentrate my self on the psychoanalytic psychotherapeutic factors of effectiveness, given by the somewhat flexible and not exactly conventional situation and way in which I work – for example, with importance to my inner frame, to be inside close to the patient/object by use of my five senses, with the help of my psychoanalytical knowing and experiences, all this always at the same time maintaining a certain inner distance, that allows me and the patient to be or to go in a process of a sufficiently independent creative living – and without initial assessments, and without my analyst's couch, and for no fee, in a humanitarian way, I see these as follows.

DOI: 10.4324/9781003451587-12

122 *What initiates psychic change and a transformation process?*

In my psychoanalytic work, here in the East African field, the basis from which I proceed is formed by my psychoanalytic concepts and thinking, and these I vary according to each situation, but never fundamentally, in order to be able to work at all in the discussed environment. I introduce into this environment a new, unfamiliar approach of viewing psychic questions, conflicts and deficiencies. I validate these in my "actions" or non-actions, by looking, listening, smelling and by using a rudimentary, clear language; and naturally by perceiving not only the phenomena, but also the deeper causes and motives, that are at work.

This may be particularly poignant and touching for patients since they have no prior knowledge of such a working together. My way of making them feel acknowledged and "recognised" is new to them and can address them deeply in their private, hidden despair, sadness, doubts, in their inner battles and deficiencies, their preconscious desires – without reference to suras or any other religion-based laws.

There is the positive attention to the narcissism of the patient by a female healer, who can be observed daily, who walks around the hospital and whose actions can be seen and can possibly also be understood. Different to conventional healers and exorcists of evil spirits, this new, female "healer" – I mean myself – performs actions that are maybe less mysterious, less scary, less threatening. Perhaps the patients I have described had already visited one or two healers before they were admitted to hospital. This is often the case with patients in the psychiatric rooms. I have, as an interested discussion partner, had talks with healers and exorcists, and I have, as a participating observer, witnessed several ceremonial exorcisms of evil spirits. During these observations, I felt extremely tense and frightened. I was scared. I felt an impulse to interfere and shout: stop this! In such ceremonies, the so-called obsessed are, seen through my Western European eyes, being severely maltreated. The reason for this is, I am told, to frighten the evil spirits into exiting the body (see Chapter 10). The aim justifies the means, it seems to me, looking at all this from my Western standpoint. The patients, the so-called bewitched, are being treated as if they were witches themselves; they apparently carry evil in them, they are considered to be contaminated. In my meetings with healers, I have had the opportunity to discuss with them their diagnostic criteria, such as criteria to differentiate between psychosis and neurosis. Their diagnostic criteria for psychosis resemble slightly those of Western diagnostics for borderline patients. At times, healers refer patients to psychiatric hospitals, and medical doctors sometimes send patients to healers. I believe that much of the diagnostics involved here springs from the healers' "practical experience". They act on intuition and have, besides the knowledge they are given by the Quran, acquired a relatively comprehensive understanding of human nature – at least the serious practitioners among them.

What initiates psychic change and a transformation process? 123

The fact that patients can observe me during my work and somehow can test me as to my harmlessness and reliability (I work under conditions and circumstances that do not correspond to the classical psychoanalytic concepts) is important to them – to be able to assess how I might, in the face of a chaotic familial environment and partly similarly chaotic hospital situation (judged by Western European standards), structure a Containing (Bion 2005a, 2005b) and perhaps a minimal Holding (Winnicott 1940a, 1940b). In all this, I think one aspect to be particularly important: for the preconscious, already the selection of patients for psychoanalytic collaboration probably represents a small act of healing, as do then the subsequent procedural steps in my approach, which are: my comprehensive view of the patient, the positive validation of his narcissism and what I address to my patients by listening, smelling, watching, looking, exchanging looks, asking and clarifying questions, meeting their needs with empathy and understanding, offering continuity in attending to them (frequently, patients see a doctor once, followed by a whole series of others they also "see" once only) and, finally, remaining available and accessible to my patients.

What exactly happens between the baby, the infant, the adolescent child, the young woman, the traumatised pregnant woman, the unhappy husband and other patients and me when transforming changes occur from the gradual dissolution into Nirvana – probably into the realm of the death drive (Freud 1920) – through to reform and the realm of the life drive?

With babies, children, adolescents, pregnant women, mothers, fathers and male patients who are subjected to various, hard to bear, traumatising situations, an understanding that takes containing functions can help like a nutritional boon and can form the basis for a potential space for self-movement and self-development. In East African orphanages and hospitals, and possibly also in European institutions, this concept is, in my experience, barely known. As a rule, the main focus understandably lies with the extreme somatic difficulties of survival.

What other, further psychoanalytic considerations are there in relation to my clinical work?

Golse says that psychic processes are already ongoing in a baby by the time it is born, and these increase in complexity over time. Golse pleads for the acceptance of the existence of a foetal psychic prenatal life – especially also to be able to work on the premise of transgenerational transmission. In the East African field, I repeat myself:

I see a strong transgenerational transmission in the form of female acceptance of, and adherence to the continuation of, the cultural norm of female genital mutilation, including acceptance of the subsequent lifelong suffering of sickness and pain.

Of course, and especially in my East African work, I base my thinking heavily on the five basic senses. In addition, I also make conscious and intensive use of the sonorous, as I already pointed out. The prenatal baby is

124   *What initiates psychic change and a transformation process?*

the only part-object that hears its mother's voice from both the inside and the outside (see Braconnier and Golse 2010; Maiello 2012). Memories of a person's earliest experiences of the sonorous can resonate and carry great worth during an entire lifetime.

D. Houzel (in Pestalozzi et al. 1998) writes:

> The newborn is in possession of psychic parts that are already born, and parts that are not yet born. The yet unborn parts of the infant's psychism are probably those that have not yet been able to be contained by the thoughts of, most likely, the mother, while the born parts of the psychism have already been contained by the thoughts of another.

This concept of "being contained by the thoughts of another" or, more precisely, I would like to emphasise, being *emotionally* contained by and in the thoughts of another, in order to be able to thrive, is of crucial importance in human development. It is also an essential building block of psychoanalytic work.

In my work, I also become this "other", who "contains" certain parts of the psychism of the babies, infants, children and adults, interprets them (by silence) and then returns them. In my work there is often only a thin line between whether or not patients give up all desires, remain in passivation (see Andre Green 2007, 2011) and withdraw into the death drive, or whether I can interest them in an exchange somehow in a uterus-like psychosomatic climate. I thereby experience often how quickly curiosity and desire can revive, as long as I can be available as an object that offers much comprehensive absorption with the necessary inner distance on my side – a psycho-economic adjustment – and for a short time acts as a good enough double (see R. Roussillon 2008).

It thereby seems to me important that the psychic, often tiniest, signs of a coming-alive during the exchange with the patient – for instance, when a patient almost unnoticeably lifted their little finger in my direction – are received in my containing and that here, in East Africa, I sometimes acknowledge this quietly in the affirmative. That is, I react and signal back, so that the patient knows that his or her signs are being received and can therefore be more and more developed. In other words, I indicate to my patients that there is a reciprocal space that connects us, a space for his or her signs which I integrate into mine and then hand back as "ours". This psychosomatic exchange, the circular nature of the encounter, is not manipulation of the other – this would be harming the other. With appropriate timing, I adapt my psychoanalytic actions to the tiniest available physical signals of the small or big "other".

All this culminates in the basically risky physical touching of exceptionally fragile premature babies, the tiniest and the tiny, and the vulnerable, scared pregnant and birthing mothers. I repeat myself: Can the smallest

What initiates psychic change and a transformation process? 125

(and the big) withstand what is being done to them? Are they calming down a little? Are they becoming livelier?

I reiterate here what I have already stated in this book about my attitude or my non-attitude: I have no goal, I am in a dreamy motion, fully concentrated and at the same time not concentrated at all, and I register what is happening at the moment or what is unfolding. I have no guiding or determining function. I do not want or desire anything. I am simultaneously doing something and not doing anything purpose-bound. This seems simple but represents one of the most challenging aspects of my work with newborns approaching death; and, of course, in my work with patients of all ages. The impulse is there to want to apply pressure – "Why don't you check the machines to monitor the success and progress of your work?" they tell me in the hospital. But I do not wish to attempt with the help of machines to become omnipotent. I understand, and try to accept, that I can fail.

Bibliography

Bion, Wilfred R. (2005a). *The Tavistock Seminars*. London: Karnac Books.
Bion, Wilfred R. (2005b). *The Italian Seminars*. London: Karnac Books.
Braconnier, A. and Golse, B. (2010). *Dépression du bébé, dépression de l'adolescent* (Le Carnet psy). Toulouse: éditions érès.
Freud, Sigmund (1920). *Jenseits des Lustprinzips*. Leipzig: Internationaler Psychoanalytischer Verlag.
Freud, S. (1926). *Hemmung, Symptom und Angst*. Studienausgabe, vol. VI. Frankfurt am Main: Fischer.
Green, André (2007). *Pourquoi les pulsions de destruction ou de mort?* Paris: Panama.
Green, André (2011). *Die tote Mutter. Psychoanalytische Studien zu Lebensnarzissmus und Todesnarzissmus*. Giessen: Psychosozial Verlag.
Hirsi Ali, A. (2015). *Reformiert euch! Warum der Islam sich ändern muss*. (Especially chapters 3 and 6.) Munich: Albrecht Knaus Verlag.
Kernberg, Paulina (2008). *Spiegelbilder*. Stuttgart: Klett-Cotta.
Maiello, S. (2012). Prenatal experiences of containment in the light of Bion's model of container/contained. *Journal of Child Psychotherapy* 38(3): 250–267.
Özdaglar, Aydan (2016). *Psychoanalytische Autorität in der Arbeit mit Patienten aus dem muslimischen Kulturkreis*. European Psychoanalytical Federation Conference, Berlin, 17–20 March 2016.
Pestalozzi, J., Frisch, S., Hinshelwood, R. D. and Houzel, D. (Eds.). (1998). *Psychoanalytic Psychotherapy in Institutional Settings*. London: Routledge.
Racamier, Paul-Claude (1993). *Le psychanalyste sans divan. La psychanalyse et les institutions de soins psychiatriques*. Bibliothèque Scientifique Payot. Paris: Payot.
Roussillon, René (2008). *Le jeu et l'entre-je(u)*. Paris: Presses Universitaires de France.
Saegesser, Barbara (2012). *Meine psychoanalytische Arbeit in verschiedenen Afrikanischen Ländern*. Basel: Psychoanalytisches Seminar Vortrag.
Saegesser, Barbara (2014). Psychoanalytische Arbeit mit BB's, Kleinkindern und Müttern in unterschiedlichen afrikanischen Ländern (Le travail psychanalytique avec les bébés, des petits enfants et des mères dans divers pays d'Afrique). *Schweizerische Gesellschaft für Psychoanalyse (SGPsa) Bulletin* No. 77 (Spring): 5–13.

126 *What initiates psychic change and a transformation process?*

Saegesser, Barbara (2015). Psychoanalytische Feldarbeit in Ostafrikanischen Städten. In: Peter Bründl and Carl E. Scheidt (Eds.), *Spätadoleszenz: Identitätsprozesse und kultureller Wandel. Jahrbuch der Kinder- und Jugendlichen-Psychoanalyse*, vol. 4. Frankfurt am Main: Brandes und Apsel: pp. 211–238.

Saegesser, Barbara (2016a). Psychoanalytische Feldarbeit in Ostafrikanischen Städten II. Elternschaft in ostafrikanischen Städten. In: Peter Bründl and Carl E. Scheidt (Eds.), *Jahrbuch der Kinder- und Jugendlichen-Psychoanalyse*, vol. 5. Frankfurt am Main: Brandes und Apsel: pp. 269–279.

Saegesser, Barbara (2016b). Un travail psychothérapeutique en marge de ma pratique psychanalytique et de la culture islamique dans des villes d'Afrique de l'est. (Translation and adaptation of my original manuscript written in German.) Lausanne. *Tribune Psychanalytique* 13.

Saegesser, Barbara (2016c). Eine Skizze psychoanalytischer Arbeit in ostafrikanischen islamischen Städten. Islamische religiös-weltliche Gesetze und Normen als Basis für Widerstand und Abwehrbewegungen von PatientInnen im Rahmen (situativ angepasster) psychoanalytischer Arbeit. *„A jour"*, 2.

Saegesser, Barbara (2016d). Koranische Normen und Psychotherapie. Lausanne. *Tribune Psychanalytique* 14.

Spitz, René A. (1945). Hospitalism: an inquiry into the genesis of psychiatric conditions in early childhood. *The Psychoanalytic Study of the Child* 1(1): 53–74.

Spitz, René A. (1948). La perte de la mère par le nourrisson: troubles du développement psycho-somatique. *Enfance* 1(5): 373–391.

Spitz, René A. (1996). *Vom Säugling zum Kleinkind. Naturgeschichte der Mutter-Kind-Beziehungen im ersten Lebensjahr.* Stuttgart: Klett-Cotta Verlag.

Spitz, René A. and Wolf, Katherine M. (1946). Anaclitic depression: an inquiry into the genesis of psychiatric conditions in early childhood, II. *The Psychoanalytic Study of the Child* 2(1): 313–342.

Winnicott, D. W. (1940a). Children and their mothers. *The New Era in Home and School* 21. Republished in L. Caldwell and H. T. Robinson (Eds.), *The Collected Works of D. W. Winnicott: Volume 2, 1939–1945.* Oxford: Oxford University Press, 2016: pp. 81–86.

Winnicott, D. W. (1940b). The deprived mother [1939]. *The New Era in Home and School* 21(3). Republished in L. Caldwell and H. T. Robinson (Eds.), *The Collected Works of D. W. Winnicott: Volume 2, 1939–1945.* Oxford: Oxford University Press, 2016: pp. 35–42.

Wohlfahrt, E. and Özbek, T. (2006). Eine ethnopsychoanalytische Kasuistik über das Phänomen der Besessenheit. *Psyche – Zeitschrift für Psychoanalyse* 60(2): 118–130.

What initiates psychic change and a transformation process? 127

Index

Note: Locators in *italic* indicate figures.

anorexia 89, 99–100, 117–119
approach adaptations, psychoanalytic-psychotherapeutic 110–111
asymmetrical parenthood 24–25

Bion, Wilfred R. 15, 21, 106, 109
boys/girls gender differences 40–42, 68–69, 69, 73, 75, 78–88, 80–81, 83, 84; *see also* female genital mutilation (FGM); parenthood; school system; sex/gender differences
Bründl, Peter 31–32

case vignettes *see* vignettes
Chasseguet-Smirgel, Janine 74
child development: female genital mutilation 42; gender opportunity/treatment differences 40–42, 68–69, 69, 73, 75, 80–81, 83, 84; narcissistic attention, affirmation 5–6, 7, 44, 45–47, 59–60; narcissistic fixation 41; play 34, 78–80, 81–82, 83, 84–88 (*see also under own heading*); sex education, sexual exploitation 87; stages 40; vignette: mother-daughter separation conflict (Na) 111–115; *see also* female genital mutilation (FGM); parenthood; school system; sex/gender differences
child transplantation 22, 29–30, 37n11, 42; case vignettes 35–36, 42–48
children's games; *see* play
containing 18, 21, 31–32, 46, 62–63, 123, 124
Coronavirus pandemic, school impact 40–41

counter-transference, transference 8, 32, 43, 44, 46–47, 92, 95, *98–99*, 107
creative play 84–85; *see also* play
customs inspection 31–32

dissociation 51, 57; vignette: survival vs environment (Z) 52–54; vignette: forced marriage, still birth (Y) 7–8
Djin / Djin exorcism 91, 92, 94, 96–99, 111, 113, 122; *see also* healer

effectiveness, psychoanalytic psycho-therapeutic factors 121–123; containing understanding, emotional containment 123, 124; inner frame, psychotherapist 121; multi-sensory communication, language 122, 123, 124; narcissistic attention 122 (*see also* narcissistic attention and sustenance); observability 123; psychoanalytic concepts 122; sonorous use 123–124
ethnology as colonial practice 93–94
ethno-psychoanalytic method 93
extended family framework 25, 43, 67, 74
external psychoanalytical frame 49–50

Fanon, Frantz 49
female genital mutilation (FGM) 12, 60, 70–76; age 42; birthing complications 29, 72; breasts 12; as girl-to-woman transformation 42, 75; male vs female circumcisions 69; mental/psychological consequences 73, 76; mother, role in 71, 74–75; physical/health consequences 29, 72, 73;

Index 129

prevalence 70, 73; as psychosomatic illness concept 60; secondary
stage 12; sexual pleasure, female 5;
third-stage (Pharaonic, la Pharaonica) 29, 60; as ultimate degradation,
physical destruction 70, 72, 74
fertility and social prestige 25–26
foetal psychic prenatal life 53, 54, 57, 58,
63, 123–124
Freud, Sigmund 15, 31, 41, 49, 52–53,
62, 70, 106

gender; *see* sex/gender differences
genital mutilation; *see* female genital
mutilation
girls/boys gender differences 40–42,
68–69, 69, 73, 75, 78–88, 80–81, 83,
84; *see also* female genital mutilation
(FGM); parenthood; school system;
sex/gender differences
Golse, Bernard 53, 62, 123
Green, André 8, 51
Griaule, Marcel 92

Hadiths 37n1, 67–68
healer, healing ceremonies 67, 91–92,
122–123; diagnostic process 95; Djin
exorcism 91, 92, 94, 96–99, 111, 113,
122; hospital vs healer choices 94,
113; Leiris on 89, 92–94, 102–103n3;
Mangas 91, 92, 95–96, 97; oral
knowledge/skill transmission 67,
92; vignette: ceremonial healer, Djin
exorcism 96–99, 97, 99; vignette:
herbal healer 95–96; Western psychotherapist (author) as 122–123
Heinrich, Hans-Jürgen 92, 94
HIV / AIDS 21, 30, 32, 36, 54–55
Houzel, Didier 62, 124
humanitarian psychoanalytical work 2;
local response, distrust or identification with colonist 50; psychoanalytic
frame (internal, external) 49–52;
psychotherapy, state of development
(East-/West-Africa) 66; Quranic
codes and individual/societal mind-
sets 66–68

in utero psychic nourishment 53, 54, 57,
58, 63
internal psychoanalytic frame 14, 15,
51–52; vignette: baby Mh 60–61
interpreters, working with 106–107

joie de vivre 4
joy: function 4–5; non-religious nature 4

Kant, Immanuel 90
Kernberg, Paulina 31
khat (*catha edulis*) 16n8, 26, 101
Klein, Melanie 8, 74

la Pharaonica 29; *see also* female genital
mutilation
Lacan, J. 32
Leiris, Michel 89, 92–94, 102–103n3
limited empathy 9; vignette, Ms A
9–10

madrasas 39–40, 67
Malinowski, Bronislaw 93
Manga 91, 92, 95–96, 97
Manichaeism 4
Médecins Sans Frontières 50, 58–60, 88
minimal holding 123
mirroring/echoing, repeating techniques 3, 51; vignette: baby Mh
60–62; vignette: Abu 58–60; vignette:
Ms A 10; vignette: Y 7–8; vignette:
young pregnant woman 36–37

narcissism, parental 26, 45
narcissism of life / narcissism of death
8, 53, 57
narcissistic attention and sustenance
5, 14, 50, 123; care staff 49–50;
children 5, 45–47, 50, 59–60;
death-to-life narcissism change 8,
10; female, mothers 5, 60, 98–99;
psychotherapeutic work, children
6, 21, 45–47; Quranic interpretation
5; vignette: unfolding healthy narcissistic traits (AB) 45–47; vignette:
narcissistic affirmation/reinforce-
ment (Abu) 59–60

orphans, orphanages: Christian
drop-in home and sexual education neglect 86–87; child handling vs care approaches 79; staff
background 80s; staff training
standards, psychotherapeutic
understanding 79; street boys
(*see* street children); Quran orphan
concept 30; vignette: withdrawal
symptoms (baby V) 99–100; vs
Western European 22

130 Index

parenthood 24–37; asymmetrical parenthood (Quran) 24–25; child(ren) transplantation 29–30, 37n11, 42; concealment of the factual, shame conflict 27–28; father role prescription (Quran) 24–25; fertility and social prestige 25–26; FGM, mothers, role in 71, 74–75; HIV / AIDS, tradition transmission impact 30, 32, 36; marital status and social acceptance 26; natural birth dogma and genital mutilation consequences 28–29; orphans concept 30; parent preferences/attachment (girls vs boys) 83; polygyny 28; practical motherhood 25–26, 47; sibling/stepsibling concept 26; theoretical fatherhood, patriarchal dominance 25–29, 28, 37n9; vs (Western) European model 24, 25, 27, 28, 30

parenthood, case vignettes: absent father trauma, enuresis, (K.) 33–35; body language, birthing 36–37; child transplantation impact, enuresis 35–36; traumatised orphan, self-fragmentation (M.) 31–32

patient selection, externally-made: knowledge-blocked patient approach 109–110; vignette: Na 110, 111–115

patient selection, self-guided 107–109; as "fresh" and "uncontaminated" encounter 109; institutional access opportunities 107; normality-to-abnormality tension 109; as reverie, dreamy gaze encounters 108, 109; vignette: B 108, 119–120; vignette: Ka 109, 115–117

"Phantom Africa" (Leiris) 92–93, 102–103n3

physical contact in psychotherapeutic treatment 110; vignette: Na 111–115

play: concept of child and play 78; family households, chores as play substitutes 80, 84; free, self-invented 83; hospital 81; international organisation institutions 88; orphanages 78–80; prayer as play substitute 83; Quranic norms 83; swimming as body-in-water play 86; toys as transitional objects 34, 78, 79; vignette: autistic orphan, boy E 81–82; vignette: El Alamein, free

play, creative world creation 84–85; vignette: play as integrational mean, shy/sensitive boy 85–86

polygyny 28, 100, 103n4

possession by evil/spirits: Djin / Djin exorcism 91, 92, 94, 96–99, 111, 113 (*see also* healer); as psychosomatic illness concept 90–91

prenatal psychic nourishment 53, 54, 57, 58, 63, 123–124

psychiatric milieu, work situation 43–44

psychic defence 5, 51, 57; vignette: dissociation, Z 52–54; vignette: HIV as defence/weapon (siblings A and T) 54–55; vignette: sensory, smell as (A) 10; vignette: dissociation (Y) 7–8

psychoanalytic frame (internal, external) 14, 15, 49–52

psychoanalytic-psychotherapeutic model/practice adaptation 110–111

psycho-narcissistic nourishment; *see* narcissistic attention and sustenance

psychosomatic illness/patients 2–3, 89–103; Djin / Djin exorcism 91, 92, 94, 96–99, 111, 113; external psychoanalytical frame 50; healers in psychosomatic care 67, 91–92, 94, 95–99, 111, 113 (*see also* healer and healing ceremonies); hospital-or-healer choices, hypotheses 94; illness as evil/evil possession concept 90–91; polygyny, effect on women 103n4; pre-natal psychosomatic conditions 53; psychosomatic thinking, Western vs East-African concepts 90–91; Quranic interpretation 90–91; theoretical unawareness, training lack 89–90; vignette: anorexic girl 99–100; vignette: withdrawal symptoms (baby V) 99–100

psychotropic drugs 91

Quran 3, 4–5, 37n1, 91; children's play 83; as code of law; code of law and unconditional behavioural expression 66–68; female genital mutilation (FGM) 75; Hadiths 37n1, 67–68; interplay with psychoanalytic thought 3, 4; male-female family dynamics, parenthood 24–28, 29 (*see also* parenthood); narcissistic

Index 131

attention 5; origins 37n1; orphan concept 30; polygyny 28, 100, 103n4; psychological processes 91; Quranic/religious-Islamic treatment resistance 6–11, 106; school system, education 39–40; self-object concept 7, 29, 91

repeating, mirroring/echoing techniques 3, 51; vignette: baby Mh 60–62; vignette: Abu 58–60; vignette: Ms A 10; vignette: Y 7–8; vignette: young pregnant woman 36–37
resistance bulwark 5
resistance to treatment; *see* treatment distrust, resistance
Ruthven, Malise 68

Save the Children 2, 88
school system 39–48; access barriers 40; child development, stages 40–41; Coronavirus pandemic 40–41; education level (East, West Africa) 38, 39, 40; gender differences 40, 41–42; High Arabic 39–40, 67; madrasas 39–40, 67; Quran influence, Quran studies 39–40, 67; rural, farmland areas 40; urban poor neighbourhoods 40; vignette: social uprooting, child transplanting (AB) 43–48
Schreiber, Konstantin 41
self (self-object, sense of) 7, 18, 28, 41, 57, 62, 85; Quran concept 7, 29, 91; vignette: AB 45–46; vignette: K 33; vignette: M 31–32
sex education 87
sex/gender differences 66–77; divorce rights and consequences 26; female genital mutilation (*see also under own heading*); female genital mutilation (FGM) 5, 12, 29, 42, 60, 69, 70–76; male circumcision 69; male progeny preference 69; marital status and social acceptance 26; patriarchal dominance (societal, family) 25–29, 28, 37n9, 70, 72; polygyny 28, 100, 103n4; practical motherhood 25–26, 47; Quranic codes and mindset forming 66–69; sex education 87; social and family treatment (boys vs girls) 41–42, 68–69, 69, 73, 75, 80–81, 83, 84; treatment imbalances 69
sexual exploitation 18

shame, therapeutical acknowledgement, validation 5, 26, 28, 35, 40, 94
scepticism about treatment; *see* treatment distrust, resistance
Spitz, René A. 53, 57
squiggle game (Winnicott) 20
street children 17–23; family backgrounds 18, 20, 21, 21–22; grand "adolescence"/ self-aggrandisement 17, 18; as-if maturity, as-if identity 18; objectifying care approaches 17, 19; psychotherapeutic drawing (technique, results) 20–23; sexual education 87; sexual exploitation, violence 18, 19; social environment and psychological development (street, market, residential home) 17–18; vignette: Christian drop-in Home, sexual education avoidance 86–87

Traditional African Medicine (TAM) 92
traditional healing methods 67, 68–69, 92, 94, 113; *see also* healer
transference, counter-transference 8, 32, 43, 44, 46–47, 92, 95, *98–99*, 107
transitional objects 34, 78, 79
translation needs as restrictive psychotherapy experience 106–107
treatment distrust, resistance 5, 106, 120; knowledgeable vs "unspoiled" approaches, patients' 106; religious-Islamic, Quranic belief-driven 106; vignette, Ms A 9–10; vignette: Na 111–115; vignette: Y 6–9
treatment length, culturally-determination of 105

unmarried mothers 42

vignettes: anorexia (girl/ girl Ne) 99–100, 117–119; child transplantation (grandmother/daughter / boy AB) 35–36, 42–48; dissociation (Z; Y) 7–8, 52–54; Djin exorcism (girls) 96–99, *97*, 99; healer (girls) 95–96, 96–99, *97*, *99*; internal psychoanalytic frame (baby Mh) 60–61; limited empathy (Ms A) 9–10; mirroring/echoing/physical touch experience (baby Mh, Abu, Ms A, Na, Y, young pregnant woman) 7–8,

10, 36–37, 58–60, 60–62, 111–115; mother-daughter separation conflict, Na 111–115; narcissistic attention, healthy narcissistic traits (AB, Abu) 45–47, 59–60; parenthood (*see* parenthood, case vignettes); play (autistic orphan, boy E, El Alamein, free play, as integrational mean shy/sensitive boy) 81–82, 84–85, 85–86; psychic defence (A, Y, Z, HIV as, smell/sensory overload as) 7–8, 10, 52–54, 54–55; religious-Islamic resistance 6–11; treatment distrust, resistance (Ms A, Na, Y) 6–9, 9–10, 111–115; self/self-object, sense of (AB, K, M) 31–32, 33, 45–46; withdrawal symptoms (baby V) 99–10

WHO (World Health Organisation) 92, 94
Winnicott, D. W. 20, 54, 58, 119, 123
Wolf, Katherine M. 53, 57

Ziegler, Jean 49

Milton Keynes UK
Ingram Content Group UK Ltd.
UKHW021707041224
451949UK00018B/354